How To

Selling to the
Public Sector

Selling to the
Public Sector

*Access and sell to the UK's
richest marketplace*

JIM GREEN

How To Books

Published by How To Books Ltd,
3 Newtec Place, Magdalen Road,
Oxford OX4 1RE, United Kingdom.
Tel: (01865) 793806. Fax: (01865) 248780.
email: info@howtobooks.co.uk
http://www.howtobooks.co.uk

British Library Cataloguing in Publication Data.
A catalogue record for this book is available from
the British Library.

Edited by Diana Brueton
Cartoons by Mike Flanagan
Cover design by Shireen Nathoo Design
Cover image by PhotoDisc
Cover copy by Sallyann Sheridan

Produced for How To Books by Deer Park Productions
Typeset by Anneset, Weston-super-Mare, N Somerset.
Printed and bound by Cromwell Press, Trowbridge, Wiltshire.

NOTE: The material contained in this book is set out in good
faith for general guidance and no liability can be accepted
for loss or expense incurred as a result of relying in particular
circumstances on statements made in the book. Laws and
regulations are complex and liable to change, and readers should
check the current position with the relevant authorities before
making personal arrangements.

Contents

List of illustrations   8

Preface   9

Part 1 – Paving the Way   11

1   **Understanding public sector business**   **11**
    What is the public sector all about?   11
    Serving the needs of the nation   11
    What you should know about public sector
        administration   12
    Appreciating demands and constraints on public
        sector servants   16
    What's in it for you?   18
    Read on and learn how to . . .   19
    Case study   20
    Exercise   20

2   **Planning ahead**   **21**
    Identifying appropriate markets within central
        government   21
    Evaluating global sectors and sub-sectors   23
    Assessing required goods and services   24
    Do you operate a management consultancy service?   24
    Checking out fitness-to-purpose   25
    Drawing up a preliminary planning strategy   26
    Is this really for you?   26
    Case study   26
    Exercise   27

3   **Prospecting and tendering for contracts**   **28**
    Where's the first place to start looking?   28
    Exploring government publications   29
    Visiting your local EuroInfoCentre   29
    Scrutinising the daily press   31

Using the Internet as a sourcing tool 31
Building your personal database 32
What is a tender? 33
Knowing when you don't need to tender 35
Case study 37
Exercise 38

4 Mastering public sector selling procedures 39
Government buyers want to do business with you 39
Mastering the procedures 40
The way in to doing business 43
Getting familiar with GPA 46
Understanding contract management 48
Be aware of the differences 49
Selling to Europe 50
Case study 50
Exercise 51

5 Selling to the public sector's biggest buyer 52
Why does the Ministry of Defence need to buy so much? 52
Where do you fit into all this? 53
Negotiating sub-contract opportunities 55
Acquainting yourself with MoD local purchasing 56
Locating construction industry opportunities 57
Exporting defence goods and services 58
Footnote on MoD trading opportunities 59
Case study 60
Exercise 60

Part 2 – The Way In 61

6 Accessing the routes for doing business 61

Part 3 – The Way Ahead 91

7 Marketing your product or service 91
What marketing is not 91
Projecting the essential you 91
How to promote in the public sector 93
Developing a niche market 94
Marketing a consultancy service 95
Drawing up your strategy 97
Case study 97
Exercise 98

8   Adding power to your negotiations   **99**
    Learning the basics   99
    Meetings and how to handle them   101
    Creative negotiation pays off   102
    Why preparation is essential in public sector negotiation   103
    Negotiating by telephone   106
    Observing signs in face-to-face negotiation   108
    Negotiating under pressure   109
    Case study   110
    Exercise   110

9   Perfecting your sales technique   **111**
    How to begin   111
    Using your powers of negotiation   112
    Prospecting for opportunities   113
    Making your appointments   113
    Face-to-face selling   113
    Ten golden rules to observe   116
    Case study   116
    Exercise   117

10 Adapting to new ways   **118**
    Keeping abreast of developments   118
    Planning ahead on all your projects   118
    Making prospecting a daily routine   119
    Watching out for procedural changes   119
    Making marketing a prime priority   119
    Developing your powers of negotiation   120
    Never lose the selling habit   120
    Continuing to learn   120

Glossary   121

Appendix   126
    Central government departments   126
    Executive agencies   127
    UK local authorities   131

Useful addresses   136

Further reading   141

Index   143

List of Illustrations

1   The divisions of government   12
2   Building on core activities   19
3   Planning ahead   22
4   Prospecting and tendering   28
5   EuroInfoCentres   31
6   Mastering selling procedures   40
7   Contract opportunities at the Ministry of Defence   54
8   Marketing   92
9   The power of effective negotiation   100
10   Sales technique   112

Preface

Throughout the seventies, the eighties and into the nineties, I spent a total of 26 years selling to the public sector. Starting with a one-off assignment for a city council, I progressed to a steady stream of contracts with departments in central and local government throughout the United Kingdom.

What I discovered right at the outset is that no matter now proficient you may be in sales and marketing, to do business successfully in this huge, dynamic marketplace, you must first acquire complete mastery of the essential procedures for selling to the public sector.

This book will show you how to go about your information gathering, how to organise your findings, and how to employ this accumulated knowledge effectively and efficiently in your quest for openings to tender and thereafter in your endeavours to compete successfully for public sector contracts.

Due to the incidence of CCT (Compulsory Competitive Tendering) all government departments are crying out for responsible new suppliers in almost every field of industry and commerce. Opportunities abound for every size of operation, from the largest to the smallest.

Selling in the public sector is fun, it's exciting, it's exacting and, for the knowledgeable player, success carries with it rewards other than mere financial gain.

Read on and learn the strategies that will access the routes to doing business.

Jim Green

PART 1 – PAVING THE WAY

1

Understanding Public Sector Business

Before we set about creating strategies and accessing routes for doing business in the public sector, let's concentrate in this opening chapter on establishing just what we're getting ourselves into – and why.

WHAT IS THE PUBLIC SECTOR ALL ABOUT?

Essentially it's about government of course, but it's also about business, big business. The **public sector** is a **marketplace** in its own right, the biggest and richest marketplace in the United Kingdom with a variety of divisions at both national and local levels. It consumes goods and services with a voracious appetite, almost everything that industry and commerce has to offer.

The marketplace we are talking about is worth billions: a market that can no longer afford to carry the luxury of the in-house provision enabling facilities it once enjoyed, a market that is now well disposed to doing business with the private sector, a market that is currently bending over backwards in its efforts to attract responsible new suppliers in every field, a market that not too many people know much about.

However, before delving too deeply into this monumental hypermart of opportunity, let's look at the various governmental functions and responsibilities which act as catalysts for the creation of the commercial opportunities we shall be examining.

SERVING THE NEEDS OF THE NATION

Compare the structure of government to that of an oak tree. The trunk is **central government**, the branches are the multiplicity of concomitant **local authorities**, and the leaves represent the plethora of specialist **agencies** which both central and local government rely on for assistance in fulfilling their respective remits to serve the needs of the nation. Central and local government and the agencies are all consumers and, in the implementation of their responsibilities to the nation, they are all armed with substantial purchasing budgets to acquire goods and services of almost every description from the private sector. That's where we come in and what this book is all about.

WHAT YOU SHOULD KNOW ABOUT PUBLIC SECTOR ADMINISTRATION

Central government

Central government goes about its business in much the same way as any commercial conglomerate. It has a chief executive (the Prime Minister), a board of directors (the Cabinet) and it holds regular board (cabinet) meetings. Its responsibilities are in the main focused on:

- defence of the realm
- economic planning
- maintaining law and order
- administering justice
- executing public and social services, including (among many others):

  – education

  – social security

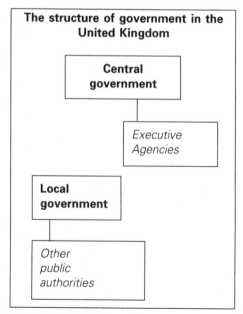

Fig. 1. The divisions of government.

- scientific research

- conservation of natural resources.

It needs ministries and departments (and purchasing budgets) to carry out these arduous tasks. Here is a complete listing of those entities of interest to you in selling to the public sector:

1. Advistory, Conciliation and Arbitration Service (ACAS)
2. Ministry of Agriculture, Fisheries and Food (MAFF)
3. Biotechnology and Biological Sciences Research Council (BBSRC)
4. British Library
5. Buying Agency
6. Cabinet Office
7. Central Computer and Telecommunications Agency (CCTA)
8. Central Office of Information (COI)
9. Council for the Central Laboratory of the Research Council (CCLRC)
10. The Court Service
11. Crown Prosecution Service (CPS)
12. Welsh Historic Monuments (CADW)
13. HM Customs and Excise
14. Ministry of Defence
15. Department of Education and Employment (DfEE)
16. Employment Service (ES)
17. Department of the Environment
18. Exports Credits Guarantee Department (ECGD)
19. Foreign and Commonwealth Office (FCO)
20. Department of Health
21. Health and Safety Executive (HSE)
22. Home Office
23. Inland Revenue
24. Intervention Board
25. HM Land Registry
26. Metropolitan Police Service
27. Department of National Heritage
28. Department for National Savings
29. Natural Environment Research Council
30. Office for National Statistics
31. Office of Water Services (OFWAT)
32. Ordnance Survey
33. Overseas Development Administration (ODA)
34. UK Passport Agency

35. Public Records Office (PRO)
36. Royal Mint
37. Engineering and Physical Sciences Research Council (EPSRC)
38. Department of Social Security (DSS)
39. Department of Trade and Industry (DTI)
40. Department of Transport
41. HM Treasury
42. The Treasury Solicitor
43. Northern Ireland
44. The Scottish Office
45. Welsh Office
46. National Health Service (NHS)
47. Higher Education Institutions
48. Local Authorities.

Examples of governmental (external) purchasing budgets
To give you a flavour, detailed below (and selected at random from the list above) are current year external purchasing budgets for goods and services from the private sector (source CCTA: Government Information Service).

Ministry of Fisheries and Food (MAFF)	£300 million
Home Office	£600 million
Intervention Board	£300 million
*Metropolitan Police Service	£397 million
NHS Supplies	£600 million
Scottish Healthcare Supplies	£450 million
Higher Education institutions	£2 billion

Enquiries from small to medium sized firms are favourably considered

Chapter 5 is devoted exclusively to selling to the biggest spender in the public sector, the Ministry of Defence (MoD). In Chapter 6 we will be looking at the goods and services on regular requirement, available budgets, and how to access routes for doing business with all the other Ministries and Departments listed above.

Local authorities
You will have observed from the main listing that the final entry, local authorities, is designated as a department of central government. That's exactly what it is, and a very important department at that. The good news is that all local authorities adopt the same principles as central government in their reception of prospective suppliers from

the private sector. Although tendering procedures may vary according to classification of council, you will approach these authorities as you would central government in your selling strategy.

Local government structure in the United Kingdom

- 34 English County Councils
- 33 London Borough Councils
- 36 Metropolitan Borough Councils
- 240 English District Councils
- 46 English Unitary Councils
- 22 Welsh Unitary Councils
- 32 Scottish Unitary Councils
- 26 Northern Ireland District Councils
- **Total** 470

That's quite a market and regardless of where you operate from, you can do business with any, many, or all of them. This is no idle claim. It's a reality that you will come to appreciate as the facts unfold on doing business in the public sector. Do your homework, create your strategy, access the route, and you can cultivate this huge marketplace to your maximised advantage.

Although there are certain variances according to classification and location of these councils, the functions and responsibilities of local authorities comprise in the main:

- Assessors/electoral registration
- Building control
- Careers service
- Cemeteries
- Cleansing
- Community education
- Consumer and trading standards
- Early years service
- Economic development
- Environmental health
- Housing
- Planning
- Roads
- Social work
- Technical services.

As you can see, there is ample scope here for doing business but it is also interesting to note the highlighted items in the 18-point aims target (detailed below) of The Local Government Association:

1. Enable all local authorities to speak with one voice.
2. Provide a national democratic leadership for local government.
3. Increase the role and influence of local government.
4. Establish better and more effective relationships with Government and the European Community.
5. Seek more control for local government over its own affairs.
6. **Raise educational standards and develop nursery education.**
7. **Regenerate local economies and reduce unemployment.**
8. **Promote safe communities free from crime and vandalism.**
9. **Promote public health, community care and voluntary services.**
10. **Ensure everyone has decent housing.**
11. **Give support to children and young people.**
12. **Protect the environment by promoting Agenda 21.**
13. Improve partnerships between central and local government.
14. **Promote value and quality in public services.**
15. Lobby to restore local financial discretion to councils.
16. Encourage more people to become involved in local democracy.
17. Demand greater powers to enable local authority initiatives.
18. Develop new models of regional government.

Even more opportunities for the discerning entrepreneur . . .

Executive Agencies, TECs and LECs

The winds of change have been blowing through the corridors of Westminster and Whitehall for some time now and this essential streamlining has resulted in the formation of new service agencies to assist government (central and local) in the fulfilment of its manifestos. These **Executive Agencies** together with **Training and Enterprise Councils (TECs)** and **Local Enterprise Councils (LECs** in Scotland) all have substantial purchasing budgets and should be added to your list of public sector prospects.

- 110 Executive Agencies
- 82 TECs
- 23 LECs

Titles for the executive agencies, TECs. LECs and all local authorities are listed in the Appendix.

APPRECIATING DEMANDS AND CONSTRAINTS ON PUBLIC SECTOR SERVANTS

Some people still look upon participation in public service as a 'cushy number'. It never was – and that's even more so today. The responsibilities are arduous and to keep astride of ever changing legislation calls for devotion to duty of a very high order. Public servants by and large work hard, know their business and in turn expect their counterparts in the private sector to know theirs. It behoves you therefore when doing business with public sector officers to do all of your homework in advance so that you fully understand the procedures essential to effecting mutually advantageous commercial transactions.

Consider some of the current demands and constraints on public servants – and the opportunities for you to shine like a beacon as a knowledgeable purveyor of goods and services to the public sector.

'Better Government'

Better Government deals with government from the point of view of the citizen, making it more effective, swifter and easier to deal with, and matching services and information more closely to the needs of citizens and the business community.

It requires 'public servants to overlay the vertical delegations necessary for accountability, efficiency and performance with horizontal linkages and incentives, necessary for government at all levels to operate in a more co-ordinated and effective way.'

But what does all this mean? It means that you can cash in if you know what you're all about.

Take the case of the Better Government attitude to information technology 'IT will help to bring government services to the citizen, rather than demanding that business and the citizen come to government.'

That's what **GIS (Government Information Service)** is about. Each and every day it beams across the Internet reams of priceless information for intelligent application by the thinking businessman.

Next Steps Programme

The **Next Steps Programme** was launched in 1988 to improve management in government and to deliver better services within available resources. It recognised the necessity for **Compulsory Competitive Tendering (CCT)** and that many essential functions undertaken in-house would now be purchased from the private sector. This decision resulted in the formation of the 110 Executive Agencies, throwing further learning curves the way of public servants, and in the process opening the floodgates of opportunity to the business community.

WHAT'S IN IT FOR YOU?

What's in it for you is precisely what you make of it for yourself. If you set about diligently applying yourself to mastering the procedures for successfully transacting business within the public sector, you will enter a market place of incredible opportunity.

Some years ago I owned and operated a marketing services agency catering exclusively for the private sector. Out of the blue one day (and resulting from a recommendation from a private sector client) there arrived an invitation to submit a proposal to the Cleansing Department of The City of Glasgow. They had been the recipients of an alarming degree of bad press on the matter of tardy collection of increasingly rancid refuse containers, the property of both local business and the local citizenry.

My first inclination was to gracefully decline the invitation on the grounds that muck always sticks. Further consideration, though, resulted in the submission of a proposed mission statement coupled with a modestly priced scattergun ad campaign featuring a cartoon character 'Captain Clean' who'd magically dashed into town to clear up the mess.

The proposal was accepted more perhaps in desperation then in good judgement. Given that the provision of external marketing services was something of a novelty in local authority circles in those days, the results were gratifying. Positive acceptance of the mission statement by the local press (possibly because the department had come 'clean' at last on its responsibilities) was matched by rapturous acclaim for Captain Clean who became so popular with the kids that a 'real' version (Ross Davidson who progressed to further fame in *Eastenders*) was seconded to trawl around schools for almost a year with his message of 'Let's clean up the city, kids'.

So what's so special about this minor and unpretentious piece of marketing?

Just this. From a single one-off bread and butter assignment I went on to attract a steady stream of increasingly lucrative commissions leading me to several more local authorities, to sundry government agencies, and eventually to the acquisition of a number of prestigious central government accounts (see Figure 2).

To quote from a DTI document on tendering for government contracts: 'Even if you are already supplying one part of the public sector, it is always worth looking for opportunities in other areas'.

I can testify to that statement – and so could you in time.

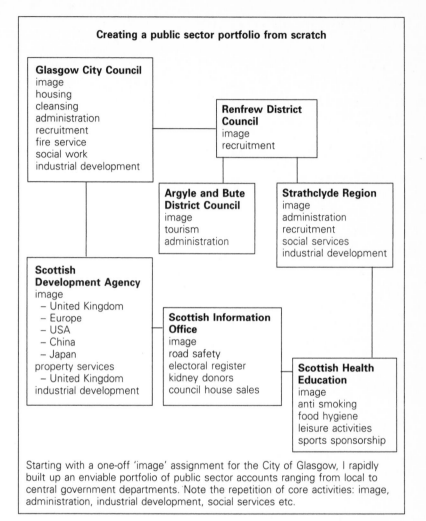

Fig. 2. Building on core activities.

READ ON AND LEARN HOW TO . . .

1. Appreciate this vast marketplace.
2. Understand the procedures required for successful negotiation.
3. Demystify the myths on tendering.
4. Locate the opportunities.
5. Identify the way in to all major departments.
6. Operate on a consultancy basis.
7. Subscribe (often free of charge) to vital publications.

CASE STUDY

Not such a daft idea

Alan and Rose are a husband and wife team operating a daily provisions service to neighbourhood factory canteens. Recently their biggest outlet closed down leaving them with an impoverished customer base. In their endeavours over a period of years to service the growing needs of this multi-national client, they had committed the cardinal error of turning away solid local business, albeit of considerably lower sales volume.

Now the multi-national had taken the money and run, and the local doors were closed to Alan and Rose. As the weeks went by, the situation had become more and more of a concern to both of them.

One afternoon Rose returned from a fruitless trawl around lapsed customers and remarked to her husband, 'I passed the Civic Centre on my way home and thought what a pity it is we can't do business there. At least there's no chance of them doing a moonlight. Daft, isn't it?'

'That's *not* such a daft idea. Maybe we should try getting some sort of contract out of them.'

'But how?' protested Rose, 'we don't know anyone in local government. There's probably forms to fill in, tendering, that sort of thing. We haven't got a clue on how to go about it.'

'Maybe there's a book at the library that could help us . . .'

EXERCISE

You are facing a similar situation to that of Alan and Rose in the case study. Due to a variety of factors, the private sector is gradually drying up on you in the way of attracting incremental business, and you are now looking around for alternative markets.

Drawing upon what you now know about the public sector marketplace, construct the beginnings of a strategy for endeavouring to sell in this vast arena.

Jot down your thoughts and keep the paper handy, or, if you have a word processor, open up a file for future reference.

2

Planning Ahead

What you need to know about doing business in the public sector is already beginning to take shape.

- You have an outline appreciation of what makes government tick.
- You know why the public sector looks to the private sector for the provision of goods and services.
- You recognise the tiers of government.
- You understand the differing functions between central and local structures.
- You have a feel for the scale of this giant marketplace.

Now is the time to make a start on your initial plan, a plan that will grow in value and stature as you progress through the chapters of this book. This is essential work that you should not defer until your induction is complete. Start today.

IDENTIFYING APPROPRIATE MARKETS WITHIN CENTRAL GOVERNMENT

Here is where to begin: set about identifying those markets most appropriate to your entrepreneurial aspirations. I'll put the focus on central government and you have your author's permission to cheat a little in the accomplishment of this exercise.

Turn now to Chapter 6. Don't read through it completely but rather scan at random the contents of several of the 48 entries. Pay particular attention to 'Locating required goods and services' and 'Accessing the route'.

Three vital factors will become apparent to you.

1. The number of times the same basic goods and services crop up under departmental requirements.
2. The inordinate assistance on offer to encourage you to become involved.
3. The plethora of useful guides you can obtain free of charge.

Take these first three vital steps on your journey

1. Draw up a list of those goods or services applicable to your particular field and note the number of departments that express a requirement for them. Concentrate solely on your random selection. Do not at this stage attempt to complete the exercise for the entire list of entries. Leave that until you reach Chapter 6 proper in your studies, by which time you will have grasped the principles of tendering, marketing and selling to the public sector.

2. Examine the various aspects of encouragement to participate in public sector business and make a note of those of particular interest. Once again stick strictly to your random selection, resisting the temptation to forge ahead through the entire contents. All you are doing right now is getting a flavour for the process of accumulating bits and pieces of vital information for future reference.

3. Choose one of the free guides on offer and write off for a copy straightaway. Upon receipt highlight the sections relating to specific requirements and the relevant tendering procedures. Don't apply for a bumper bundle of these tomes of wisdom. You can do that later if you wish when you've absorbed the full content of Chapter 6.

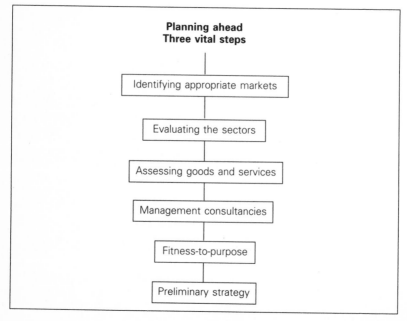

Fig. 3. Planning ahead.

EVALUATING GLOBAL SECTORS AND SUB-SECTORS

Let the learning curve direct you now to an initial evaluation of the various sectors and sub-sectors which combine to form the enormous marketplace which is the public sector. We know that the core comprises:

- 48 ministerial/departmental outlets
- 470 local authorities

  add to that

- 110 Executive Agencies
- 82 TECs
- 23 LECs

  add for good measure. . .

- 44 police authorities in England, Wales and Northern Ireland
- 52 passenger transport authorities
- 11 National Parks

Adding to your plan

Now add to your plan by executing the following directives in your own time as you progress your studies. Success in selling to the public sector comes through knowledge which is only acquired by assiduous information gathering. You'll be doing a lot of that before you set out to land those big revenue contracts. It's the only way because there are no shortcuts to actualising achievement in public sector business.

- Increase your knowledge of each sector and sub-sector, concentrating on one at a time.

- Start first with central government and you'll find all you need to know about that in Chapter 6.

- Next tackle local authorities and for that you'll need a copy of *Municipal Yearbook & Public Services Directory* (see Appendix or visit your local reference library).

- Spend some time browsing through a copy of *A Guide to the Executive Agencies* (see Appendix or visit your local reference library).

- Visit your nearest TEC or LEC which will be happy to provide you with appropriate literature.

- Back to the reference library and devote some time to the *LGA (Local Government Association) Yearbook* where you'll find useful information relating to police and passenger transport authorities.

- Refer to the Appendix for details of National Parks locations and contacts.

- Use reference library photocopying facilities rather than indulging in laborious note-taking.

- When you have completed your global appraisal, create your very own local digest comprising central government regional offices, local councils, Executive Agencies, LECs/TECs, police authorities, passenger transport authorities, etc situated within a 50-mile catchment area.

- Concentrate your information gathering on this local digest for the time being.

ASSESSING REQUIRED GOODS AND SERVICES

It is not too early to have a stab at establishing where your own range of goods or services fit into the general scheme of public sector requirements. Staying with central government and referring back to the notes you made in Vital Step 1, apply the same criteria (linking merchandise/service to requirements) to the various entries in your newly created local digest. At this point you have no way of knowing for sure who buys what, how, when, where or why – but you can be sure they do. Store this information and we'll look again at how to use it to effect in the next chapter.

Feel free to dig deeper right now if you wish. For example, if you want to know more about what's on offer at your local council(s) and you're on the Internet, go to the UK local government web site. Every day more and more councils are creating their own web pages, which invariably contain a smattering of invitations to tender. Your council(s) may already be among them.

DO YOU OPERATE A MANAGEMENT CONSULTANCY SERVICE?

If so, you will notice that references to consultancy services in all the entries in Chapter 6 are lacking in precision and definition. Don't be put off by these seeming omissions.

Management consultancies are in ever-increasing demand by the public sector and, by any measurement, it is a huge market for consultants. Although actual revenue figures are not available, it could be worth as much as £1 billion per annum.

Information technology accounts for around 50 per cent of the total market but there are many other areas where management consultancies obtain commissions on a regular basis:

- business process re-engineering
- change management
- corporate finance
- efficiency reviews
- executive search/selection
- facilities management
- financial management
- human resources
- marketing
- market research/surveys
- policy development
- privatisation
- project management
- quality
- strategy and planning
- training.

You may be looking at a few hours/days of expert consultation on a specific issue, or involvement in a major multimillion-pound project of year(s) long duration.

Using your professional judgement and local knowledge relating to civic matters, you can at this stage make an educated guess as to where your particular expertise links up to as yet unprescribed management consultancy opportunities within your own immediate area of public sector activity.

More on management consultancies and the public sector in Chapter 7.

CHECKING OUT FITNESS-TO-PURPOSE

Evident though it may be, let's talk for a moment about *why* we're indulging in this appraisal. To safeguard fitness-to-purpose there are two factors on which we require absolute assurance.

- That we are connecting all possible links between known goods/ services and known public sector requirements.

- That we are not missing out on possible opportunities elsewhere in the spectrum.

The first part is easy but perhaps we need to apply a degree of lateral thinking to the second part to obtain best advantage in the long term. Discount nothing. There will be areas right now where your menu doesn't apply – but maybe it will in time. You may want to branch out into these areas or you may decide to sub-contract to someone who can do what you currently canot do.

Pro-activity is essential if you are to make your way in the public sector.

DRAWING UP A PRELIMINARY PLANNING STRATEGY

I thrive on lists: things to do, things accomplished, things to forget, projects on the go, projects abandoned etc. Here's a list for you – your preliminary planning strategy.

1. Make information gathering on public sector matters a daily routine.
2. Start with central government and move on.
3. Identify your markets.
4. Break them down into sectors and sub-sectors.
5. Link your product/service range to prescribed requirements.
6. Check out where you could be doing business right now.
7. Check out where you could develop future opportunities.

IS THIS REALLY FOR YOU?

Now is the time to stand up and be counted. Hopefully you can see where all this is leading and that you will stick with it to the end. Competing in the public sector carries with it rewards other than financial: it's stimulating, it's fun, and it's a continuous learning exercise from which you will glean a great deal of valuable information which will serve you well in your private sector dealings.

CASE STUDY

Searchlight on the public sector

A partners' meeting was taking place at Searchlight, an ambitious, up-and-coming executive search consultancy. They had reached the item on the agenda where suggestions were being called for on extending the client base.

'What about the public sector?' volunteered one of th
members.

'Challenging, even for us, wouldn't you say?' countered one of
seniors. 'It's massive. Anyway, what isn't handled in-house is mo
likely already sewn up. Old cronies, that sort of thing.'

'Highly unlikely,' contributed another member. 'Nowadays, considerations on tenders other than of a strictly commercial nature are
deemed unlawful.'

'I think it's an excellent suggestion,' assessed the senior partner,
who looked in the direction of the enterprising junior as he contin-
ued, 'How do we go about it?'

'Make a start right here in our local patch. I'll fix up an exploratory
meeting with the Director of Human Resources at the District
Council. I'll give him a mini presentation to break the ice.'

'Good thinking . . . and when you've done that, pop round to the
reference library. They're bound to have directories on central government departments, executive agencies. . .'

The search at Searchlight had begun in earnest on sourcing additional markets.

EXERCISE

Go back to the exercise you began in Chapter 1. Dig out the piece
of paper or refer to the computer file and extend your strategy from
what you've just added to your knowledge of doing business in the
public sector.

3

...ıg and Tendering for Contracts

This chapter addresses **prospecting** for openings and **tendering** for contracts. It is too early to take up any offers yet, but the exercise will add valuable grist to information gathering.

WHERE'S THE FIRST PLACE TO START LOOKING?

Right here where you are. When the time comes that you're looking around in earnest for openings, start first with your local digest and (hopefully beefed up) preliminary planning strategy. Time will have moved on and perhaps by then an opening may present itself from

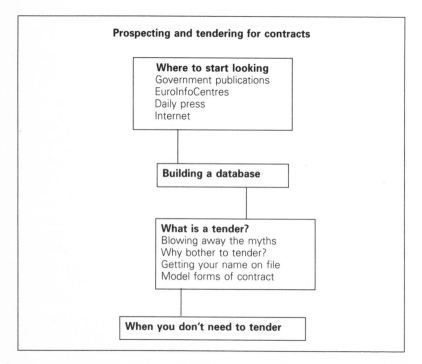

Fig. 4.   Prospecting and tendering.

your accumulated findings, an opening which may lead to an invitation to tender, and in time to a contract

Remember it only takes one piece of business to get you going, and remember too the DTI injunction to look for similar opportunities in other areas of the public sector. Once you get a foot in the door and start providing value for money, reliability, consistency and continuity, news of your good works will spread and you will quickly build up increasing elements of trust, confidence and satisfaction among central and local government departments.

EXPLORING GOVERNMENT PUBLICATIONS

Attention to these journals is essential if you are to be a major player. They provide the means of keeping abreast of current opportunities, tenders open to offer, possible future purchases, single source contracts awarded, competitive contracts awarded, together with snippets of useful advice for potential suppliers.

Most popular and best read among these are:

- *Government Opportunities*
- *Official Journal of the European Communities*
- *Ministry of Defence Contracts Bulletin.*

Subscription details in Useful Addresses.

Increase your knowledge by studying the free 'selling to . . .' guides

If you haven't yet done so, write or telephone now for one or two of these highly informative booklets. They will give you a flavour for sourcing possible openings and they all contain helpful guidance on specific required procedures. Also included in many of them are contact details for current and future use.

VISITING YOUR LOCAL EUROINFOCENTRE

Maybe you think it's too early yet to be thinking about European involvement . . . but there again, maybe not. Perhaps you'll find your first opening there, your first tender, and your first contract – and it might just be on your own local patch.

The **EuroInfoCentre** initiative was established by the European Community in 1987 to create the 'first stop' source of European business information. Serving private sector companies across Europe, there is now a network of over 230 EuroInfoCentres providing *full* *access* to the latest information on opportunities for the business community.

Here are just a few of the services you can use free of charge.

Tenders Electronic Daily (TED)

Tenders Electronic Daily (TED) gives you up-to-the-minute details on more than *600 public sector tenders* published every day. It covers contracts in both mainland Europe and the United Kingdom. With TED you can tailor the search to match your own commercial sector, geographical location or specific awarding authority. Daily output is available by e-mail, disk or hard copy.

Visit your nearest centre soon and take full advantage of this incredible free offer to source initial openings.

Weekly Bulletin

This EuroInfoCentre weekly newsletter highlights core issues in European policies, legislation, funding programmes, initiatives, and it regularly features forthcoming European related events. You can select those items of prime interest to your enterprise or you can order the full text.

Alert Service

Adapted to your specific requirements, **Alert Service** keeps you up-to-date with new and amended guidelines, regulations and legislation as these matters affect your sector.

Grantfinder

Once you are up and running and doing business in the public sector, **Grantfinder** could prove useful should you consider that your enterprise could benefit from grant funding. The service will guide you quickly and easily through the welter of available (and sometimes otherwise confusing) funding information to identify the European and UK grant schemes best suited to your needs.

Grantfinder provides you with the choice of one-off searches or monthly updates according your business and financial profiles.

Business Co-operation Service

The time will arrive sooner than you think when you could be looking for a European business partner who is also involved in selling to the public sector. **The Business Co-operation Service** can advertise your profile on the electronic network of over 400 correspondents in Europe and abroad.

Connecting Europe
with your Business

EuroInfoCentre Ltd

Fig. 5. The EuroInfoCentre initiative was established by the European Commission in 1987 to create the First Stop source of European business information.

Market intelligence

Using the most extensive databases available, coupled with the EuroInfoCentre network of contacts, you have the opportunity to analyse your potential global market. Too much to take in when you are only considering sourcing openings for invitations to tender? Don't you believe it. The more you know, the better prepared you will be to participate successfully.

SCRUTINISING THE DAILY PRESS

Not only the quality broadsheets but also the popular tabloids (especially regional) carry reams of classified advertisements for both central and local government opportunities to tender. Spend an hour or so at your local reference library to determine on which days particular newspapers feature these treasure troves of opportunity.

USING THE INTERNET AS A SOURCING TOOL

The scope of the Internet as a worldwide research and sourcing tool improves and expands every day, as does the quality of the content.

If you are not yet connected to the World Wide Web, then try out the system on a browser at your neighbourhood public lending library and make your first port of call CCTA/GIS (Central Computer and Telecommunications Agency/Government Information Service) which features a remarkably efficient search facility. This is a superb public sector learning curve of which you should take early advantage.

Next go to the local government web site and progress from there on to as many individual council sites as you can manage. Suggestion: see if any of your local councils have web sites. That way you'll get an inkling as to how progressive they are in their own marketing.

For those of you who are already online, download those pages of particular interest. Don't dig too deeply into the Internet research facilities just yet though – we'll look again in the next chapter at just what a marvellous aid to selling it can be.

BUILDING YOUR PERSONAL DATABASE

As the information gathering process increases its momentum, you will want to co-ordinate these findings into an orderly sequence so that crosschecking is easy. Using the content of your already created local digest as the starting point, choose between these options:

- manual recording
- electronic application.

Manual recording
Not everyone is entirely comfortable with the new technology and if you fall into this category, that's okay. Just make sure that you use only one journal to record all your information. Scattering it around in a profusion of notebooks will only irritate you when what you need to know straightaway sets you off on a paper chase.

Classification
Classification is important for ease of reference and some page headings immediately spring to mind:

- Central government regional offices in your area (locations/contacts/tel/fax/e-mail)
- Local authorities (ditto)
- Executive Agencies
- TECs/LECs

- EuroInfoCentre
- Other relevant public bodies
- Tenders documentation:
  - press cuttings
  - Internet print-outs
  - TED hard copy.

You'll think of other headings once you get started.

Electronic application
Organise your data in much the same way as you would if you were doing it manually and clearly label all your computer files. Have back-up for everything you record.

Daily updating
This will be vital when you're into the swing of public sector involvement. Don't let the day end without reviewing and updating your files – manual or electronic.

WHAT IS A TENDER?

In essence, a tender is an offer to supply goods or services (or both) on predetermined conditions. In the context of the public sector, basic conditions of tender will include commitment to:

- value for money
- assurance of quality
- stipulated delivery.

There will be other conditions of tender which will vary according to the nature of the proposition.

Blowing away the myths
Lots of people in commercial practice talk lots of rubbish about the process of tendering. There's no old boy network at play in the public sector, no favouritism, no cronyism, no back scratching. As the character in the previous chapter's case study intimated, that would be unlawful. Considerations other than those of a strictly commercial nature are taboo in public sector tendering.

Look at it as you would when chasing for business in the private sector. Fred Fernackapan runs a one-man joinery business. He needs new letterheads, so what does he do? He picks up the telephone and calls for three quotes. Fred is asking for tenders but it's certain he's going to give the order to the lowest bidder.

That's *not* the way it works in the public sector. Price alone won't get you there. Compliance with the three factors listed above constitutes the basic criteria.

Why bother tendering?
Simple. If you're not in, you can't win. The process of tendering is fair, the rules for entry are laid down, and everyone competing has the same opportunity for success.

Getting your name on file
Here's something you can do to build a nest of prospects for the future. If you are committed to doing business in the public sector, if you have confidence in your products or service, if you can see a connection between what you have to offer and what they require, then compose a well couched letter of introduction and send it off now to all of the entries in your local digest. Tell them who you are, where you are, what you are and what you do. Ask them if they currently use your type of product(s) or service. Wait for a week or so, and irrespective of whether you receive replies or not, telephone and ask for an appointment.

Here's the good news. You'll get that appointment much sooner and much more easily than you would if you were applying the same technique to cold prospects in the private sector.

Model forms of contract
The **Central Unit on Procurement (CUP)**, who produce a regular series of guidelines on purchasing and supply procedures for government departments (central and local), recently introduced three **model forms of contract** which can be used for most procuring purposes. The model forms cover these essential requirements:

- goods (excluding computer hardware and software)
- general services
- consultancy services (excluding works or capital projects).

They are models of simplicity and although their use is not mandatory, all departments are encouraged to adopt these forms in general practice because of the fact that the **purchase order** becomes a key document in the contract.

Content of the model form of contract
- purchase order number
- supplier details

- delivery/service requirements
- payment terms
- authorisation.

Simplicity itself ... to make it easier for you to do business with government departments.

KNOWING WHEN YOU DON'T NEED TO TENDER

There are two recurring circumstances where you are not obliged to go through the tendering process to sell to the public sector.

- local purchases
- transactions based on perceived value.

Local purchases

Certain local purchase contracts (where the monetary consideration is minor) are awarded solely on the submission of an acceptable quotation. This is an area of opportunity open to small traders of good repute.

Transactions based on perceived value

(Q) When is a tender not a tender? (A) When it's a proposal.

There are situations where the commercial sector has something of monetary value to offer the public sector but for which it does not expect direct financial reward in return. Unlikely proposition perhaps, but it does happen. One classic example (of which I have had some experience) is **sponsored publishing**. It works like this: the publisher makes an offer (by way of a proposal) to supply an agreed quantity of publications (local guides; street maps or atlases; planning, building control, or environmental information handbooks etc) in return for the granting of exclusive advertising rights by the local council or other public authority concerned. Printing and production costs are recovered from the advertising revenue obtained and the residue represents the publisher's profit.

Sounds good, but don't rush into it. Even the most seasoned practitioner can take a bath on this one. Look around though if the idea appeals to you. There are other opportunities of doing business in the public sector on transactions based wholly on perceived value.

Extraneous opportunities for general traders

Although perhaps not entirely appropriate to this book, there is another area where you can do business indirectly in the public sector – as opposed to *selling* directly to it. It's an area of particular interest to general traders and one capable of producing handsome dividends.

Government auctions are conducted nationwide on a regular basis, from various sources, and for a variety of reasons:

- government surplus
- HM Customs and Excise
- police
- bankruptcy and liquidation
- plant and machinery
- transport
- on-site sales
- US Government Department of Defense.

Government surplus
Auction sales of UK Ministry of Defence and Home Office goods that are surplus to requirements: vehicles, computers, tools, hardware, school and hospital supplies, nationalised public utility service machinery, generators, clothing, uniforms, furniture, local authority property and land, etc.

HM Customs and Excise
Auction sales of impounded merchandise – from the effects of convicted drug traffickers and racketeers to lost and found dinghies. Also included in these sales are goods confiscated in lieu of duty and those seized at ports and airports.

Police
Sales of unclaimed, lost, stolen and recovered possessions – bicycles, household electronics, jewellery, office equipment, car stereos, cell phones – 'Aladdin's caves' – the contents of which are auctioned regularly. Buy from the police cheaper than you could from the criminals!

Bankruptcy and liquidation
Sales of the seized assets of companies in receivership/administration – goods which are auctioned for whatever anyone is prepared to pay. Hundreds of sales every month for all types of goods.

Plant and machinery
Specialist sales via agents who deal exclusively in printing machines, farm equipment, photographic equipment, computers, electronics, mechanical goods, vehicles etc.

Transport
Sales of lost and unclaimed personal effects – from umbrellas by the thousand to handbags, briefcases, overcoats, filofaxes, wallets, books etc. Also included are sales of airport lost property.

On-site sales
Liquidation/relocation auctions of stocks that are too vast or bulky to be moved – those which take place on the premises or at trading sites and thus occur at different venues every week.

US government Department of Defense
Surplus sales that take place regularly in the UK and throughout Europe – new and used merchandise which comprise everything imaginable required to service the needs of the modern armed forces.

Buying at auction
To give you a flavour of the bargains achievable, look at these prices recently fetched at auction:

Item	*Retail price*	*At auction*
Porsche	£22,000	£7,560
Bedroom suite	£500	£27
Pioneer hi-fi	£500	£20
Canon photocopier	£3,000	£240
E-Type Jaguar	£6,000	£3,500
Miele washing machine/dryer	£600	£3

You don't have to tender when participating in government auctions and your prospecting is restricted to monthly reviewing of *Government Auction News* which you can subscribe to by applying to GAN, Freepost, Romford RM6 5BR.

CASE STUDY

Charles and Maurice agree to differ
Charles was pleased but Maurice didn't share his brother's enthusiasm. Their recently launched marketing consultancy had just

completed its first contractual assignment for the local Health and Safety Executive, and Charles was looking for more.

'That was strictly a one-off,' decreed Maurice. 'They won't be back and even if they are it will only be with another £20 job. We'll do much better concentrating on the private sector.'

'I wouldn't be too sure about that. Gaining some early kudos in the public sector could do us a lot of good in the other place ...'

'Okay, so how would we go about it?'

'The Health and Safety Executive are happy with results of the first project. They've told us so, and in writing.'

'So?'

'So, we contact all the other departments in the council and tell them what clever clogs we are.'

'How?'

'I'll write a letter of introduction.'

EXERCISE

Go back to your preliminary plan and your newly extended local digest. Take them both with you (hard copy if yours is an electronic compilation) on your visit to the EuroInfoCentre. Record everything that proves of initial interest to you and open up a special section on Tenders Electronic Daily (TED).

Your plan is now beginning to take shape.

4

Mastering Public Sector Selling Procedures

We have a grasp on how to go about prospecting for openings and a smattering of knowledge on the process of tendering for contracts. What we must do now is learn to master the accepted procedures for selling in the public sector, and how we will achieve this is by viewing matters from the perspective of our opposite number in the equation, the buyer of our goods and services.

When you arrive at the point where you have to prepare written proposals and engage in face-to-face selling, you must be able to demonstrate that you have a clear understanding of these procedures and you can only do that if you have mastered them in advance. There is nothing difficult about any of this because the procedures are simple, workable and easy to comprehend. All you have to do is to learn them and apply them intelligently.

GOVERNMENT BUYERS WANT TO DO BUSINESS WITH YOU

The aim of this chapter is to lay out these essential procedures as plainly as possible. In the process, it will give you the background on how public sector purchasing is organised and where to go for further information. To begin, read this extract from the DTI booklet (URN 98/603) *Tendering for Government Contracts*:

> Public bodies spend a vast amount each year on goods and services. They are always looking for new suppliers. Whatever the size of your business, there are always opportunities to supply this market.

How's that for motivation?

Not only is there a huge market out there and opportunities for everyone, and not only are the purchasing budgets substantial – but government goes out of its way to make it easy for you to do business with them. If you need further motivation, read this second extract from the same document:

> Even if you are already supplying one part of the public sector, it is always worth looking for opportunities in other areas. The public sector includes

central government departments, local authorities, the National Health Service, and the academic institutions, so there is plenty of scope for business.

MASTERING THE PROCEDURES

Let's examine the procedures we are to master. We will break down the relevant background data into manageable chunks.

- general principles
- notes for small business concerns
- sub-contracting
- private finance initiative
- the way in to doing business
- purchasing procedures
- types of contract
- contract conditions
- payment on time
- cautionary advice.

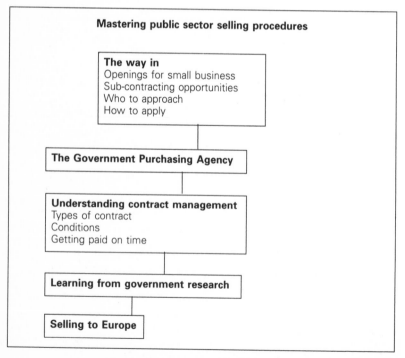

Fig. 6. Mastering selling procedures.

Familiarise yourself with these principles
As a general rule, all public sector contracts are subject to the Treaty of Rome, irrespective of value. The Treaty sets down principles to prevent discrimination against concerns, firms, companies from other Member States and promotes the freedom to provide goods, services and workers throughout the European Community.

The Treaty is reinforced by a series of EC procurement directives which are implemented into UK law by the Public Works Regulations 1991, the Utilities Supply and Works Contracts Regulations 1992, the Public Services Contracts Regulations 1993 and the Public Supply Contracts Regulations 1995.

What does all of this mean for you? It means that these regulations establish procedural rules which set down non-discriminatory and transparent criteria for the selection of tenderers and the award of contracts with a value above the relevant threshold. (Details of the current level of these thresholds may be obtained from your local EuroInfoCentre or from *Government Opportunities*). In essence, everyone starts on the same level playing surface when tendering for public sector contracts.

Opportunities for small firms to get involved.
Nowadays there are lots of excellent opportunities for small firms to do business with government. Departments are not required to buy through central suppliers and are accordingly able to save money by purchasing direct from suppliers. These departments are becoming increasingly aware of the advantages of placing contracts with small firms.

Remember, though, that government buyers are always seeking value for money and to become a successful supplier you must demonstrate:

- ability to compete with other firms.
- ability to complete contracts on time and to the required standards.
- evidence of a sound financial and commercial reputation.
- ability to familiarise yourself with government purchasing procedures.

When it's best to opt for sub-contracting opportunities
Central government departments and local authorities do not normally deal in component parts or materials, nor do they select sub-contractors (they expect their main contractors to assume this responsibility).

Therefore it follows that if you only produce components, your best bet is to look for opportunities as a sub-contractor. Names of the main contractors are at the rear of the booklet *Tendering for Government Contracts*, a copy of which you can obtain from:

DTI Publications Orderline
Admail 528
London SW1W 8YT
Tel: (0870) 1502 500. Fax: (0870) 1502 333.

Consider PFI if you're among the big boys

To date the primary focus has been on *services* sold to the public sector and in particular, major projects where companies in the private sector assume responsibility for the upfront investment in capital assets.

Through the **Private Finance Initiative** (**PFI**) the private sector is able to contribute a wide range of managerial, commercial and creative skills to the provision of public services, offering potentially huge benefits to participating government departments.

These are the three main types of PFI transactions:

1. Services sold to the public sector where the public sector pays only on the delivery of specified services to prescribed quality standards. Often acting in consortia, the private sector aims to reap synergies across DBFO (design, build, finance and operation).

2. Financially free-standing projects where the private sector undertakes DBFO, recovering costs entirely through direct charges on the private use of the asset (for example: tolling) rather than from payments by the public sector whose involvement is restricted to enabling the project to proceed through assistance with planning, licensing and other statutory procedures.

3. Joint ventures where the costs of the project are not met wholly through charges on end users but are subsidised from public funds. In many instances the public sector secures wider social benefits.

PFI transforms government departments and their agencies from being owners and operators of assets into purchasers of services from the private sector. Private firms become long-term providers of services rather than simply upfront asset builders, combining the responsibilities of DBFO in order to deliver the services demanded by the public sector.

To give you an indication of the scale of PFI, by April 1997 contracts for £6.8 billion of private finance projects were signed.

Publications including the guidance document *Partnership for Prosperity* are available from the Public Enquiry Unit of HM Treasury.

THE WAY IN TO DOING BUSINESS

In the previous chapter we looked briefly at ways of sourcing openings to tender. Now we look fully at these avenues, in particular the Internet and how it can help us locate opportunities.

The Official Journal of the European Communities
The vast majority of procurement contracts worth more than a specified threshold must be published in the daily supplement of the *Official Journal of the European Communities*. This supplement provides details of current contracts, invites suppliers to tender (or to express intent of interest) and publishes information about contracts already awarded. Tender invitations are listed by directive and summary data is supplied for each commercial opportunity.

You will need elements of the new technology to access this daily supplement if you require information in a hurry.

- CD-Rom
- The Internet
- Scanfax.

CD-Roms
These are produced either twice or five times a week, and are available on subscription from The Stationery Office or from the Office for Official Publications based in Luxembourg.

Tenders Electronic Daily (TED)
This is the online version of the *OJ* which provides complete daily information on invitations to tender for public contracts. Reports are available to subscribers of this monitoring service on the morning of their publication. TED offers the advantage of being highly selective, using subject and country codes to provide users with direct access to notices in their field of interest. It also gives out data on some below-threshold opportunities. TED is available to you at your local EuroInfoCentre.

Scanfax

The Stationery Office also operates a **Scanfax** service which is just one of a number of scanning services that will fax specific extracts from the *OJ* to subscribing customers.

However, if you are not in a hurry or you're not yet on the Internet, there is another means of access open to you: hard copies of the *OJ* are available from certain central libraries and local chambers of commerce.

Areas of opportunity on the Internet

The Internet abounds with channels of information on public sector matters but there is one web site in particular to which you should pay an early visit: **BIP** (**Business Information Publications**). Try out the free demos on each of the following and see for yourself how many opportunities you can locate in just one viewing:

- *MoD Contracts Bulletin* featuring service and supply requirements for the Ministry of Defence.
- *Contrax Weekly* announcing opportunities for the supply of goods, materials, services, and works requirements of central and local government; health, police, fire authorities; education boards; utilities and off-shore exploration companies.
- *Project* spotlighting software for the electronic production and transmission of public sector contract notices and tender information.
- *Public Sector Property* dealing with open contracts for works, services, goods and materials relating to property within the public sector.
- *Tracker*: the complete daily electronic contract information search service.
- *Government Opportunities* showing the way into contract opportunities for service requirements within central and local government and NHS Trusts, plus information relating to PFI, competition and government agencies.

Lists of potential suppliers

Most firms interested in doing business with the government need to be accepted onto a department's list of *potential* suppliers. In certain instances, though, this is not necessary, eg where a contract is valued at less than £10,000.

If you are accepted onto one of these lists, don't anticipate that you will be asked to tender straightaway because you won't necessarily.

Opportunities in the press

Just to remind you ... scan the press regularly for opportunities to tender in your field:

- national press
- regional newspapers
- trade magazines
- *Government Opportunities*.

Knowing who to approach

Chapter 6 deals with this subject in detail, providing you with access routes, department by department. When you've identified your particular route and write off to express intent of interest, your abilities will then be matched to the requirements of the various contracts divisions within that department. After that, you will be given an idea of the sort of information they need from you.

How to apply

Always ensure that you state your case clearly in your written application by including the following:

- Description of your products/services in simple, non-technical language.

- Complete range listing so that your application may be circulated to a wide variety of purchasers.

- Client list detailing any large companies, public bodies, foreign governments with whom you've done business.

- Outline of any assignments you have undertaken for UK government departments in the past.

If you get a result ...

Should your application attract some interest, you'll be asked to complete a questionnaire (unless your interest lies solely in small value contracts) and inspectors may also visit your premises to discuss the enterprise more fully. They'll want assurance that your business is financially sound and that it has the ability to handle contracts to the required standard and to effect completion on time.

If you don't ...

If you are unsuccessful, endeavour to establish whether you provided the right information and indeed, whether you approached the right department. Ask why your application didn't succeed. This will help you the next time you apply.

Quality assurance

Very often government departments will express a requirement to assess contractors against certain **quality assurance** standards. If you operate in an industry where external assessments are the norm, and if it is appropriate to a particular contract, then you are likely to find this a requirement.

ISO 9000

Government procurement agencies encourage their suppliers to adopt the ISO 9000 quality standard, and added confidence in a company's abilities can be achieved if the supplier seeks independent, third party assessment of the system in operation.

GETTING FAMILIAR WITH GPA

The **Government Purchasing Agency (GPA)** is a commercially orientated professional purchasing executive which was created to ensure fair and open competition for government business. It focuses on close working relationships with the private sector, resulting in improved competitiveness and value for money in all departmental commercial transactions.

Numbered among the GPAs clients are:

- Department of Finance and Personnel
- Department of Environment
- Department of Agriculture
- Department of Health and Social Services
- Department of Education
- Department of Economic Development
- Northern Ireland Office.

Viewing matters from the buyers' perspective, GPA provides the following services for its customers:

- Establishing that contracts are awarded in compliance with procurement legislation.
- Overseeing purchasing contract management.
- Advising on procurement including major capital projects.
- Training in effective and efficient procurement.
- Complying with EC directives and other procurement services.

Conversely, and from our viewpoint, the GPA adheres to its own **Suppliers Charter Statement** which provides all suppliers with the opportunity to compete for the provision of goods and services in fair, open and equal competition. This statement also sets out the rights of existing or potential suppliers.

Suppliers Charter Statement
Under the terms of this charter, all suppliers have a right to:

1. An equal and fair opportunity to compete for business on the basis of the principles of European Union (EU) purchasing legislation. Competitions will be publicly advertised, as appropriate in the *Official Journal of The European Union* and local/national press. Full information on the timetable for each procurement, the process to be used, and the mandatory requirements will be provided to all those responding to the appropriate advertisement.

2. Non-discriminatory specifications setting out customer requirements and incorporating International, EU or British Standards, or equivalent, as appropriate.

3. The opportunity to propose innovative cost effective alternatives, if appropriate, which satisfy specifications.

4. Encouragement to deliver goods and services which are environmentally friendly.

5. A fair evaluation of competitive bids taking account of pre-determined criteria, for example quality, service, price, economic advantage. All bidders will be kept informed on the progress of evaluation, which will be conducted as soon as possible.

6. Notification of the outcome of competitions in which they have an interest. Appropriate contract award notices will be published in the *Official Journal of the European Union*.

7. Feedback, to be given on request, where a bid has been unsuccessful. De-briefing will include reasons for failure, whilst respecting commercial confidences.

8. Prompt payment as required by government and contractual obligations and in line with the Prompt Payer's Code of the CBI. Invoices should be paid within 30 days of receipt.

9. Expect courtesy and respect and all enquiries to be dealt with promptly, efficiently and to the highest professional standards.

It will be to your advantage to learn and master the principles laid out in the GPA Suppliers Charter Statement. Note in particular the reference to *quality, service, price, economic advantage*. The Government Purchasing Agency, like all other public sector entities, is the custodian of public funds and as such has a duty always to endeavour to obtain the best value for money in the open marketplace.

The Government Purchasing Agency is a friend to guide you in your quest to doing business in the public sector.

UNDERSTANDING CONTRACT MANAGEMENT

Government departments place contracts for a great variety of work and if you are to be a regular recipient of such contracts, it is important that you understand the **contract management** concept.

The process of contract management ensures that all parties to a contract fully comprehend their respective obligations, enabling these to be fulfilled as efficiently and effectively as possible to provide even better value for money all round. This process runs from initial identification of the need to completion of the contract. It has two core objectives:

* Management of the relationship between client and supplier.
* Identification, allocation and management of the risks associated with the performance of the contract.

Types of contract
These are the five main areas where government places contracts with the private sector.

1. research and development
2. production of equipment
3. supplies for stores
4. general services
5. local purchase orders.

Framework agreements or **call-off contracts** are common and are based on an estimate of a department's total requirement over a stipulated period. Orders are placed when the need arises during the period of the contract.

Conditions of contract
The majority of government contracts are constructed around model documents, which may vary slightly from one department to another.

There may also be other distinctions where special needs are required.

Comprehension of the conditions upon which these contracts are based is vital for new entrants into public sector selling.

- these documents constitute a two-part set
- part one consists of the general conditions you will find in any contract
- part two contains a series of specified additional conditions if the contract warrants them.

There are three model forms of contract, which can be used for procuring:

1. goods
2. general services
3. consultancy services.

For smaller contracts, simple standard forms are often used by departments.

Getting paid on time

All government departments are obliged to pay promptly in accordance with agreed contract terms and the norm is within 30 days of receipt of a valid invoice. Make sure then that your invoices are correct and on time, every time.

Point to note: any changes made during the period of the contract should be agreed in writing and any other changes (business name, address etc) should be advised to the appropriate department.

More detailed information on payment terms is published by the Department of Trade and Industry in its booklet *Better Payment Practice* which is available from DTI Publications Orderline.

BE AWARE OF THE DIFFERENCES

Clearly there are many distinct advantages in doing business with the public sector but it is equally to your advantage to be aware of the differences in this market.

You must acknowledge that bidding procedures will be more testing since (unlike the private sector) their aim is at all times to ensure value for money for the taxpayer.

Government researched feedback from previously successful suppliers strongly recommends that you:

- Be persistent in searching for information.
- Use available sources of information to assess the market.
- Do not wait for government buyers to come to you.
- Find out where invitations to tender are published.
- Get your name onto relevant tender lists where opportunities are *not* published.
- Do not rely on trade gossip.
- Ensure that you fully understand the buying requirements before tendering.
- Ask for (and learn from) feedback if your tender is unsuccessful.

The moral is: be proactive in all of your endeavours.

SELLING TO EUROPE

The Single Market has created opportunities galore for *firms of all sizes* to compete for public sector contracts across Europe. There is a requirement on all government departments, both in the UK and the rest of Europe, to advertise certain types of public work. Bear in mind though that, while this provides you with greater scope to do business abroad, you may equally have to compete with other European firms for contracts in the United Kingdom.

CASE STUDY

Efficiently, effectively and on time . . .

Roofing specialists Raft & Company received an invitation in the morning mail to tender for a major works project involving three local NHS Trust hospitals.

The principal gathered his troops together later than afternoon to discuss how best to prepare and present a winning proposal. 'We know what we're all about,' he began, 'but do we really know enough about this project to fulfill the requirements efficiently, effectively and on time? I doubt it.'

'Then let's call an early meeting with the signatory of the letter of invitation,' suggested the next in command.

'Oh, we'll do that for sure,' replied the principal. 'However, we've got some preliminary work ahead of us before any meeting. Some R and D. Research what we don't know about public sector procedures so that we can develop our strategy and produce a meaningful proposal.'

'Do we have the time for all of this?' enquired another colleague tentatively.

'We'll make time. These people are mustard on contract management. Let's show them we know as much as they do about the subject. On the matter of research ... I bags the Internet ... Who's up for the field stuff?'

EXERCISE

Devise a scenario for handling an initial meeting with public sector officials on the matter of contract management relating to a project in your own field of commercial activity, the contract for which you have just been awarded.

List all the salient factors that are likely to arise during the discussion and devise appropriate strategies for addressing each in turn.

5

Selling to the Public Sector's Biggest Buyer

Having examined in detail (and hopefully mastered) public sector selling procedures, let us now put the focus on marketing goods and services to the single biggest spender among government departments.

The Ministry of Defence (MoD) has an annual budget of around £12 billion for the purchase of goods and services. Much of this expenditure goes the way of multinationals but the MoD also buys from sole traders and the smallest of limited companies. They don't just buy, they buy big from the largest to the smallest supplier. Nobody in the United Kingdom spends more and nobody can match their range of requirements.

WHY DOES THE MINISTRY OF DEFENCE NEED TO BUY SO MUCH?

There are lots of reasons. Consider for example, the quarter of a million service personnel stationed throughout the world. These servants of the Crown need:

- clothing
- food
- housing
- furniture
- furnishings
- cleaning and cleansing services
- sports facilities.

The MoD also requires equipment for essential services:

- medical
- dental
- fire.

MoD vehicles require:

- fuel
- servicing
- spare parts
- replacement.

MoD administrators require:

- office equipment
- telecommunications
- stationery
- computer hardware and software.

MoD researchers require:

- laboratory equipment
- technical back-up services.

MoD bands require:

- instruments
- sheet music.

The list of MoD requirements is endless and the Department takes its responsibilities to the taxpayer very seriously. Over 1,000 buyers are committed to purchasing high quality goods and services at the most economical prices. But price isn't the sole criterion for doing business with the Ministry of Defence. Quality and fitness-to-purpose are equally important.

WHERE DO YOU FIT INTO ALL THIS?

If you are in business, almost any kind of business, you ought to seriously consider the MoD as a customer. They will in their turn welcome your interest and reward it with helpful assistance in a variety of ways which we will examine in detail throughout this chapter.

To encourage UK traders who look to the MoD as a potential market for their goods and services, the **Defence Suppliers Service (DSS)** was set up to provide information and help. The DSS responds rapidly to enquiries from traders and it takes its message to industry at seminars, exhibitions and 'meet the buyer' events at locations throughout the country. It provides:

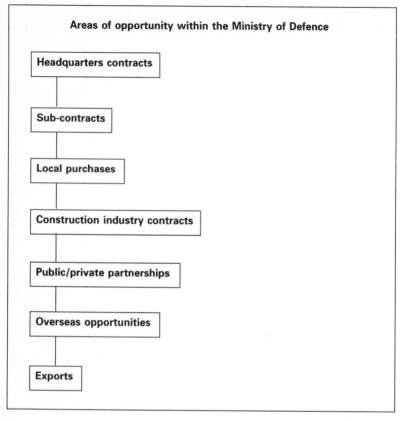

Fig. 7.   Contract opportunities at the Ministry of Defence.

- helpful assistance
- rapid response to enquiries.

Cultivating MoD headquarters contacts

Herein lies the nub of MoD purchasing power. Headquarters place several billion pounds worth of contracts with prime contractors every year, covering a wide spectrum of goods and services. These contracts range from orders for jet aircraft to requisitioning supplies of paper clips.

There are buying offices located throughout the UK, placing approximately 45,000 *new* contracts each and every year. If you were successful in landing one of these contracts you would be at liberty to sub-contract some of the load but you would equally be responsible for total supervision of the entire project.

The opportunities are there and if you can satisfy the MoD that your standards are as high as theirs, you will be considered as prime contractor material. Match MoD standards and you can anticipate fair terms, prompt payment and even on occasion interim payments:

- contracts awarded annually worth billions
- MoD buying offices are located throughout the United Kingdom
- option to sub-contract
- fair terms
- prompt payment
- staged payments by arrangement.

How to make initial contact

In the first instance, subscribe to the MoD *Contracts Bulletin* (see page 59), a fortnightly digest which is a valuable source of information to would-be suppliers. The content includes tenders invited; tenders awarded; announcements on possible future purchases etc. It is worth noting here that, in the not too distant past, to be invited to tender for the majority of headquarters contracts your company would have been required to be on the MoD Defence Contractors List (DCL). Nowadays however, because of the MoD's increasing reliance on third-party quality assurance, your company's credentials are acceptable as long as they appear in the Department of Trade and Industry's (DTI) Register of Quality Assessed Companies.

Always bear in mind that it's not necessarily the biggest that are awarded the best contracts. If your company is qualified to meet MoD tendering criteria, then it is equally qualified to be awarded a contract.

NEGOTIATING SUB-CONTRACT OPPORTUNITIES

As a direct result of the many new headquarters contracts awarded annually, there are a vast number of sub-contract opportunities available in a huge variety of goods and services.

The good news here is that, if you know what you're about, the MoD adopts an 'eyes on – hands off' policy with regard to the negotiation of sub-contracts. They prefer to leave it to the prime contractor to ensure that the MoD's policy of competitive tendering and long-term value for money is carried out efficiently. The MoD also deems it vital that a prime contractor's in-house elements should compete for all aspects of the work against the capabilities of external supply sources.

- New contracts = sub-contract opportunities.
- 'Eyes on – hands off' policy eases the way to successful negotiation.

How to learn about opportunities
Subscribe to *Works Services Opportunities* (published fortnightly) which lists all project management and term commission contracts. It also provides details of future opportunities, contracts awarded and current contracts together with informative articles and valuable contact reference points.

Tip: if you are interested in being invited to tender for construction contracts, you are advised to register on the New Qualification System (NQS) administered by the Department of Environment, Transport and Regions.

ACQUAINTING YOURSELF WITH MoD LOCAL PURCHASING

Ministry of Defence local purchase offices have a remit to deal direct with suppliers in purchasing goods and services for the daily running of the units under their control.

The majority of local purchase orders will be for a few hundred or a few thousand pounds. These orders represent good opportunities if you are in business in a small way. Prove that you can guarantee value for money and, as with headquarters contracts, you will receive fair terms and prompt payment.

How to get involved
The procedures are informal. Most MoD local purchase offices use directories to locate suppliers. Get yourself to the forefront by making your services known by submitting a well-couched letter outlining relevant goods, services and capabilities. Don't mailshot these offices, whatever else you do, and make sure that your introductory letter asks a core question such as, 'Does your unit currently buy my type of product of service?' This will establish at the very outset whether or not a ready-made market exists.

You will find that many of the lower value orders are placed with the minimum of formality with often no more than oral or faxed tendering involved.

A list of local purchase sites is available from the Defence Suppliers Service.

LOCATING CONSTRUCTION INDUSTRY OPPORTUNITIES

At both national and local levels, construction and property management work is covered by the Defence Estate Organisation (DEO). This section is in turn broken down into sub-sections covering projects, sub-contracting, term commissions and property management.

What does DEO mean by 'projects'?

Projects are defined as work with a construction cost in excess of £240,000 (including fees and VAT). The DEO prepares a brief and appoints a project manager who is capable of managing the entire construction process from procurement and responsibility for the design, through to site supervision and handover.

Term commissions for **project management** are awarded on a competitive basis for periods of between two and three years. If you are interested in project management, bear in mind from the outset that the DOE will only appoint firms that can demonstrate multi-disciplinary skills. For example, architects are better advised to concentrate on term commissions or sub-contracting opportunities.

What are 'term commissions'?

Term commissions are placed on an area basis to provide advisory services to the Defence Works Advisor. These services may involve: initial assessments, order of cost estimates, option studies, condition surveys and project brief preparation. Term commissions can also be placed to provide specialist work on behalf of property managers and/or as support to specialist staff within DEO.

Looking out for sub-contracting opportunities

In the case of projects, many sub-contracting opportunities exist for both consultants and construction firms. Project managers are allowed to buy in the services of architects, engineers and quantity surveyors. Likewise for construction, prime contractors need sub-contractors to supply everything from site security to plant and machinery.

Openings at local level in property management

Every MoD unit or establishment has a works service manager who, under the terms of contract, is obliged to invite tenders for all work valued at more than £5,000. This creates many sub-contracting opportunities at local level.

How to find out more about construction contracts

Subscribe to the fortnightly digest *Works Service Opportunities* which lists all project management and term commission contracts together with details of future opportunities, contracts awarded and current contracts. Each issue also includes articles and useful contact points.

Footnote on quality assurance: The MoD places great importance on quality standards and always aims to place contracts with companies which meet the requirements of BS EN ISO 9001. Sub-contractors, however, need not necessarily be BS EN ISO registered.

Considering public/private partnerships as an alternative

The MoD encourages innovation and more flexible contractual relationships in achieving best value, and **public/private partnerships** form an essential element of the wider efficiency agenda.

Details of plans and proposed projects are published in the MoD *Contracts Bulletin, Government Opportunities* and where appropriate, the *Official Journal of the European Communities.*

EXPORTING DEFENCE GOODS AND SERVICES

The United Kingdom, as a member state of the European Community and a signatory to the Agreement on Government Procurement (GPA), has to meet certain international obligations relating to public procurement which are intended to open up the market within those countries and provide open and fair competition.

Some other European nations publish their own contracts bulletins, details of which can be found in the MoD *Contracts Bulletin.*

The obligation to open UK contracts to overseas companies has a complementary requirement for overseas companies to admit UK suppliers. The daunting prospect of keeping abreast of changing foreign import laws and international trade agreements can deter even the most determined exporter. The Defence Export Services Organisation (DESO), which is part of the MoD, complements the wider export services offered by the Department of Trade and Industry. DESO offers its invaluable expertise and knowledge to British companies wishing to export defence products and services. Its advisory services are provided free of charge.

As the focal point within Whitehall for all defence exports matters, DESO:

- briefs companies new to defence exporting
- advises on worldwide, country and regional market opportunities
- provides military assistance to support defence exports

- sells surplus UK equipment, spares and stores (opportunity here for small traders)
- helps UK companies to obtain export licences
- advises on defence export finance
- organises defence exhibitions, inward missions and equipment demonstrations
- negotiates and manages UK MoD's Industrial Participation (IP) agreements.

FOOTNOTE ON MoD TRADING OPPORTUNITIES

Of the three essential MoD digests to which you have already been referred in this chapter, the most frequently read is *Contracts Bulletin*. Before signing off on opportunities to trade with the MoD, let's examine the content headings that appear in a recent issue:

- index (itemised descriptions of all items in 44p edition)
- introduction (featuring golden snippets of advice to potential prime contractors)
- announcements (seminars, reports, etc)
- possible future purchases
- tenders invited
- single source contracts awarded
- competitive contracts awarded
- addendum (lots of useful tips and reference points here)
- facilities management procurement in the MoD.

Here is an example of one of the 'golden snippets' featured in the announcements section under the banner headline 'Advice for New Suppliers'.

> The Ministry of Defence spends over half its budget each year on equipment, works and miscellaneous stores and services, ranging from tanks, ships and aircraft, through to tools, clothing, window cleaning, and much more besides. To get the best value for money we are encouraging more new suppliers of all sizes – including small firms – to compete for defence business. Are you interested? If so, the MoD's Defence Suppliers Service (DSS) will be delighted to hear from you.

What does the DSS offer?

- Easily accessible focal point for enquiries.
- Free advice and assistance to all new suppliers on how to sell to the MoD.

- Signposting services. If you need specialist advice they can put you in touch with the right people.

Details of how to subscribe to all MoD publications are given in Useful Addresses.

CASE STUDY

Good reports on Tommy's acumen

Tommy owns a small company that provides security guards to private sector concerns throughout North Yorkshire. One day out of the blue he received a communication from the Works Service Manager of a local Ministry of Defence establishment enquiring whether his company would be interested in tendering for the supply of security personnel on a project with a contract span of two years.

Tommy discussed the invitation with his foreman who expressed reservations about the company's credentials for making an acceptable tender.

'Waste of time, I reckon. It's all about quality assurance nowadays. They'll want us to be BS EN ISO registered, and we're not.'

'Maybe you're right, I don't know ... but I think I'll make some enquiries anyway.'

Tommy did enquire and to his relief was informed that sub-contractors were exempt from BS quality assurance registration.

He tendered for the work, was successful, and later discovered that the works service manager had made the initial approach on the basis of good reports he had heard about the company's performance in the private sector.

EXERCISE

Write a letter of introduction to your local MoD purchasing office outlining:

- your company's range of goods/services
- its capabilities
- its commitment to quality assurance.

6

Accessing the Routes for Doing Business

Having progressed thus far in your studies on how to follow proven strategies and access the routes to successful selling in the public sector, you will by now have:

- gleaned an understanding of public sector business
- engaged in some pre-planning
- looked around for initial openings
- acquired basic knowledge on tendering and contracts
- applied yourself to mastering the procedures for selling successfully
- learned how to approach the biggest spender in the public sector
- started to formulate your own strategies.

Here comes the interesting part, something to whet your appetite for what's to follow. With all of the foregoing information at your disposal, you are now ready to take an in-depth look at essential research data on the high spending central government ministries and departments. These research findings will direct you to:

- individual departmental requirements for goods and services
- purchasing budgets (where available)
- the routes for doing business.

ADVISORY, CONCILIATION AND ARBITRATION SERVICE (ACAS)

If you think this is an unlikely candidate to head the list of prospects, then you're wrong. ACAS is a substantial independent statutory body whose essential responsibility is to promote the improvement of industrial relations throughout the United Kingdom and, as such, needs a variety of merchandise.

Locating required goods and services
Everything connected with an office-based environment.

Accessing the route
Finance and Purchasing Manager, ACAS, Brandon House, 180 Borough High Street, London SE1 1LW.

MINISTRY OF AGRICULTURE, FISHERIES AND FOOD (MAFF)

MAFF has a network of purchasing staff in not only the core department but in its executive agencies as well. The engine room (Procurement and Contracts Division) applies the 'competing for quality' criteria within MAFF and sets national agreements for the supply of many merchantable items.

Annual purchasing budget: £300 million.

Locating required goods and services
- advertising
- research and development
- agricultural machinery
- facilities management
- consultancy
- animal foodstuffs
- building management
- printing
- computer hardware and software
- office machinery
- office cleaning
- furniture
- protective clothing
- telecommunications
- laboratory consumables
- photographic equipment
- veterinary products.

Accessing the route
If you would like to sell to MAFF you should first write to request a copy of the booklet *Selling to MAFF* which contains a wide range of useful contacts and sundry helpful guidance. Copies may be obtained from Procurement Contracts Division, Ministry of Agriculture Fisheries and Food, Room 820a, 19–29 Woburn Place, London WC1H 0LU.

BIOTECHNOLOGY AND BIOLOGICAL SCIENCES RESEARCH COUNCIL (BBSRC)

This is one of six such councils empowered to fund a specific area of science undertaken by research institutions and universities. The offer to provide various goods and appropriate consultancy services is open to the private sector.

Accessing the route
Procurement Section, BBSRC, Polaris House, Swindon SN2 1UH.

BRITISH LIBRARY

In its national operations the British Library provides comprehensive reference lending, bibliographic and sundry other services based on its vast collection of books, maps, music, periodicals, sound recordings and other materials.

Locating required goods and services
- stationery
- computer software
- cleaning
- office equipment
- telecommunications
- catering
- office furniture
- consultancy services
- computer hardware
- maintenance.

Accessing the route
Interested suppliers should contact: Contracts and Purchasing Unit, The British Library, Boston Spa, Wetherby LS23 7BQ. Tel: (01937) 546000.

THE BUYING AGENCY

This is an essential agency of which to take particular note. It provides procurement services for a wide range of goods and services related to the domestic and operational needs of government departments and other public sector bodies.

Locating required goods and services

- accommodation services
- building interiors
- environmental requisites.

- healthcare
- fuel and energy

   Contracts are normally awarded on the best value-for-money-over-time basis, taking into account all aspects of cost-over-time including capital, maintenance and operating costs, *not merely the lowest price.*

Accessing the route

Write to the undernoted office which will also provide you on request with a useful booklet entitled *Selling Through the Buying Agency.* The Buying Agency, Royal Liver Building, Pier Head, Liverpool L3 1PE. Tel: (0151) 227 4262.

THE CABINET OFFICE

To efficiently manage a modern office-based organisation, the Cabinet Office and the Office of Public Service (OPS) need to buy many goods, pieces of equipment and services. Purchasing is devolved within the central department and to the five OPS executive agencies which provide specialist services to the Civil Service.

Locating required goods and services

Cabinet Office and Central OPS

- Information technology including personal computers, applications software and development, fileservers, operating systems, network equipment and data cabling.

- Office stationery and non-IT equipment including fax machines, photocopiers and dictation machines.

- Property management services: building works and maintenance including painting and decorating, minor building and demolition, joinery, electrical services and window cleaning.

- Furnishings including carpets, curtains, sofas and cushions, desks, chairs and non-security cupboards.

Executive agencies

Civil Service College
- information technology
- audio visual equipment
- educational supplies
- books
- periodicals
- publications.
- printing
- publicity

Property Advisers to the Civil Estate
- personal computers
- network equipment
- system analysts/programmers
- fileservers
- data cabling
- IT project managers
- facilities management
- fax machines
- desks
- hardware maintenance
- photocopiers
- chairs
- wide area network
- dictation machines
- filing cabinets
- telecommunications
- carpets
- cleaning facilities
- office stationery
- curtains and blinds.

Security Facilities Executive (SAFE)
- Vehicles,
- security equipment,
- contracting services,
- security furniture,
- administrative items.

Accessing the route

If you are interested in supplying any of the above divisions, write to the relevant contact (see below) who will provide you with details of the tendering process. Include a copy of your catalogue together with a price list.

Note: contracts are invariably let through competition and requirements above certain *de minimus* price levels are advertised in *Government Opportunities*. Contracts with a value above the relevant EC threshold are advertised in the *Official Journal of the European Community*.

Cabinet Office and Central OPS
Information Technology: Cabinet Office, ITSB, Horse Guards Road, London SW1P 3AL.
Office stationery: Cabinet Office, Horse Guards Road, London, SW1P 3AL.
Property management: Central Accommodation Manager, Cabinet Office, Queen Anne's Chambers, 28 Broadway, London SW1H 9JS.

Civil Service College, Sunningdale Park, Larch Avenue, Ascot, Berkshire, SL5 0QE.
Information Technology: IT Manager.
Facilities management related equipment and services: Facilities Manager.
Library items: Librarian.
Printing and publicity: Strategic Marketing Manager.
Other products and services: Finance Officer.

Property Advisers to the Civil Estate
Contracts Manager, St Christopher House, Southwark Street, London SE1 0TE.

Security Facilities Executive
Director of Finance Executive and IT, St Christopher House, Southwark Street, London SE1 0TE.

CENTRAL COMPUTER AND TELECOMMUNICATIONS AGENCY (CCTA)

CCTA is responsible for promoting the effective use of information systems in support of efficient delivery of business objectives and improved quality of services by the public sector. It develops and produces best-practice advice and guidance on all aspects of planning, management and implementation of information systems for its clients.

Accessing the route
Write to CCTA, Rosebery Court, St Andrews Business Park, Norwich, NR7 0HS.

CENTRAL OFFICE OF INFORMATION (COI)

This is the executive agency that provides publicity services to government departments and publicly funded organisations. Apart from the London headquarters, there are eight regional offices covering England. One of the country's biggest advertisers, around 85 per cent of **COI**'s purchasing budget is spent with external suppliers of which it has over 5,000 on its books. The majority of these are *small firms* or *individuals* who provide a wide range of publicity related services.

Locating required goods and services
- advertising
- direct marketing
- market research
- publications
- electronic media.
- films
- exhibitions
- conferences
- promotions
- journalism
- photography
- translations

Accessing the route
All enquiries should in the first instance be addressed to:
Purchasing Officer, COI, Room 151, Hercules Road, London (020) 7261 8302.

COUNCIL FOR THE CENTRAL LABORATORY OF THE RESEARCH COUNCIL (CCLRC)

The chief function of CCLRC is the support of Research Council funded scientific, engineering and technology programmes.
   Annual purchasing budget: £50 million.

Locating required goods and services
- engineering plant
- office machinery
- stationery
- engineering equipment
- IT supplies
- printing
- building works
- IT maintenance
- electrical equipment
- civil engineering
- IT software
- electronics

- lasers
- scientific equipment
- publications
- gases
- optics
- site services
- chemicals
- furniture.

Accessing the route

Write, telephone or fax: Procurement Group, CCLRC, Rutherford Appleton Laboratory, Chilton, Didcot, Oxfordshire OX11 0QX. Tel: (01235) 446589. Fax: (01235) 445794.

THE COURT SERVICE

The Court Service is responsible for the staffing and running of all the civil and criminal courts in England and Wales (except Magistrates' Courts).

Locating required goods and services

- stationery
- office furniture
- consultancy assignments
- office machinery
- information technology.

Accessing the route

Office supplies: The Court Service, Procurement Unit, 2nd Floor, Southside, 105 Victoria Street, London SW1E 6QT.
Information technology: The Court Service, ISD2, Southside, 105 Victoria Street, London SW1E 6QT.

CROWN PROSECUTION SERVICE (CPS)

The remit of the CPS is the independent review and conduct of criminal proceedings instituted by police forces in England and Wales.

Locating required goods and services
- catering
- communications equipment
- print
- cleaning
- consultancy services
- stationery
- computer hardware
- furniture
- telecommunications
- software and consumables
- furnishings.

Accessing the route
If you are interested in supplying CPS either centrally or locally, write to: Purchasing Unit, Crown Prosecution Service, Headquarters, 50 Ludgate Hill, London EC4M 7EX.

HM CUSTOMS AND EXCISE

HM Customs and Excise has offices throughout the United Kingdom and is divided into 14 regional areas, which are referred to as **Collections**. There are also headquarters offices in London, Liverpool, Manchester and Southend.

Purchasing organisation

Departmental Purchasing Unit
DPU is a central unit responsible for purchasing policy, providing support and advice and undertaking major purchasing projects.

Central Purchasers
Some larger value or more technically complex purchases (mainframe computers, vessels and major construction projects) are handled by specialised headquarter locations in conjunction with the DPU.

Local Purchasers
Local managers in each of the 14 Collections have the authority to purchase the vast majority of their own goods and services. While they use centrally generated contracts for some of these requirements they also buy more general items from local and regional suppliers.

Locating required goods and services

- telecommunications
- furniture
- instruments
- office machinery
- office cleaning
- sampling equipment
- stationery
- minor works
- marine fittings
- printing
- uniforms
- repairs and maintenance.

Accessing the route

If you consider your organisation could be a potential supplier to HM Customs and Excise, or you want to obtain more precise information regarding tendering for their contracts, write to the address below and request a copy of *Selling to HM Customs and Excise* – an extremely helpful guide for all potential suppliers.

HM Customs and Excise, Ralli Quays, Stanley Street, Salford, M60 9LA. Tel: (0161) 827 0267. Fax: (0161) 827 0270.

WELSH HISTORIC MONUMENTS (CADW)

CADW is an executive agency whose role is to protect, conserve and promote an appreciation of the built heritage of Wales.

Locating required goods and services

- general construction projects (main and sub-contract)
- cleaning services
- small plant
- grounds maintenance
- maintenance services
- landscaping
- print
- consultancy services
- exhibition design and organisation.

Accessing the route

Interested suppliers should contact the Procurement Section and be prepared to provide complete details regarding their company's capabilities. If you are interested in this one, you will also be asked to fill in a supplier appraisal questionnaire.

Procurement Section, CADW: Welsh Historic Monuments, Crown Building, Cathays Park, Cardiff CF1 3NQ.

MINISTRY OF DEFENCE (MOD)

The Ministry of Defence is the biggest purchaser in central government and there are three main ways in which firms can win defence work:

- direct headquarters contracts
- local purchase orders
- sub-contracts from main defence contractors.

(See Chapter 6 for complete details on selling to the biggest spender in the public sector.)

Accessing the route

Defence Supplies Service, Maple 2B#22, MoD (PE) Abbey Wood, PO Box 702, Bristol BS12 7DU. Tel: (0117) 91 32843/32844

DEPARTMENT FOR EDUCATION AND EMPLOYMENT (DfEE)

The DfEE operates from four major sites at Sheffield, Darlington, Runcorn and London. Commodity-based teams do most of the purchasing which consists of the usual spread of office equipment and services. DfEE has no special requirements.

Accessing the route

Send details of your services to DfEE or telephone PCD1 (CPU) who will transfer your call to the appropriate buying team.

PCD1 (CPU), Room N1106, Moorfoot, Sheffield S1 4PQ. Tel: (0114) 2594024

EMPLOYMENT SERVICE (ES)

The ES has two head office contracting and procurement units.

Locating required goods and services

- security
- catering
- stationery
- print
- building maintenance
- computer consumables
- office furniture
- information technology
- consultancy services.

Accessing the route

These goods and services are normally acquired through competitive tendering and consequently the ES does not hold or maintain a central list of potential/approved suppliers from which it exclusively invites tenders. The regional teams are also responsible for letting and managing a number of other contracts solely for their region.

Head of Estates & National Contracts Manager, Division Head Office Purchasing Unit, 1st Floor, Porterbrook House, 7 Pear Street, Sheffield S11 8JF

Head of Process & Systems Division, Process & Systems Team 4, Procurement Unit, Steel City House, West Street, Sheffield S1 2GQ.

DEPARTMENT OF THE ENVIRONMENT (DOE)

The DOE has a role in promoting best procurement practice within the construction industry and leads on purchasing by Government Offices for the Regions.

Locating goods and services

- information technology
- office machinery
- printing
- stationery
- office furniture
- uniforms.
- protective clothing
- consultancy services

Accessing the route

Write to the Procurement Adviser listed below who can also provide you with the booklet *Selling to the DOE* together with an environmental guide for potential suppliers of goods and services to DOE.

Principal Procurement Adviser, Department of the Environment, Room C4/09, 2 Marsham Street, London, SW1P 3EB.

Alternatively telephone the Procurement Policy Unit on (020) 7276 6016 or (020) 7276 6174 for further information.

EXPORT CREDITS GUARANTEE DEPARTMENT (ECGD)

ECGD is a small government department with offices in London and Cardiff.

Locating required goods and services

- audio-visual equipment
- consultancy services
- publications
- building maintenance
- office furniture
- stationery
- catering and cleaning services
- furnishings
- telecommunications
- software and consumables
- printing
- uniforms.

Accessing the route

Contracts are normally placed as a result of competitive tendering. Apply in writing to:
Director of Purchasing, ECGD, PO Box 2200, 2 Exchange Tower, Harbour Exchange Square, London E14 9GS. Tel: (020) 7512 7171. Fax: (020) 7512 7649.

FOREIGN AND COMMONWEALTH OFFICE (FCO)

Some FCO purchasing departments are located in central London but the main centres for purchasing are Croydon and Milton Keynes.

Accessing the route

Enquiries about FCO Procurement may be made by telephone or in writing to:
Purchasing Directorate, 1 Palace Street, London SW1E 5HE. Tel: (020) 7238 4743.

DEPARTMENT OF HEALTH

This department purchases a variety of goods and services mostly by competitive tender.

Accessing the route

Write to: Department of Health, RMF-RM2: Purchasing Unit, Room 608, Richmond House, 79 Whitehall, London SW1A 2NS. Tel: (020) 7210 5629.

HEALTH AND SAFETY EXECUTIVE (HSE)

The aim of the HSE is to ensure that risks to people's health and safety from work activities are properly controlled.

Locating required goods and services
- building maintenance
- furniture
- stationery
- office machinery
- information technology
- scientific equipment.
- cleaning

Accessing the route
Enquiries regarding the supply of goods and services should be addressed to:
Health and Safety Executive, Purchasing and Supply, Room 506, St Hugh's House, Trinity Road, Bootle, Merseyside L20 3QY. Tel: (0151) 951 4081. Fax: (0151) 951 4291.

HOME OFFICE

The Home Office and its agencies consume a wide range of goods, services and works. There are also over 150 establishments throughout England and Wales with powers to meet some of their needs locally. Examples: prisons and police training centres.

Annual purchasing budget: £600 million.

Locating required goods and services
- office machinery
- scientific equipment
- maintenance
- office equipment
- laboratory equipment
- consultancy services
- information technology systems
- construction.

Accessing the route
The Home Office has produced an informative booklet entitled *A Suppliers Guide*. Copies of this and further information about supplying the Home Office may be obtained from:
Room 963, Home Office Procurement Unit, 50 Queen Anne's Gate, London SW1H 9AT. Tel: (020) 7273 2717. Fax: (020) 7273 2404.

INLAND REVENUE

There are several opportunities for businesses to tender for contracts for goods and services with the Inland Revenue. Contracts are awarded after competitive tender procedures and while some small contracts may be let at local level, the vast majority of significant value are now on centrally negotiated call-off contracts. Don't allow this to put you off though, because the opportunities are still there to do business at all levels.

Locating required goods and services
- printing
- office consumables
- estate management
- IT equipment
- office equipment
- hotel accommodation
- stationery
- furniture
- catering
- conference accommodation
- consultancy services
- security
- cleaning.

Accessing the route

Goods and services
Inland Revenue, Contracts and Procurement Unit, Block 1 Government Buildings, Kingston By Pass Road, Surbiton, Surrey KT6 5QR. Enquiries to CPU Help Desk. Tel: (020) 8268 4321.

Facilities management
Inland Revenue, Contracts and Procurement Unit (Facilities Management), Mowbray House, PO Box 55, Castle Meadow Road, Nottingham NG2 1BE. Enquiries to Robin Davey. Tel: (0115) 974 0407.

IT equipment
Inland Revenue, Business and Management Services Division, 10 Maltravers Street, London WC2R 1LB. Enquiries to Paul Peck. Tel: (020) 7438 7233.

INTERVENTION BOARD

The Intervention Board is a Next Steps Agency which implements EC legislation regulating the market for many agricultural products and foodstuffs.

Annual purchasing budget: £300 million.

Locating required goods and services

- processing facilities
- storage facilities
- information technology
- cleaning
- printing
- office machinery.
- stationery
- furniture

Accessing the route

Enquiries about tendering for goods and services (other than those related to IT, building services and accommodation) should be directed to:

Procurement and Supply Services, Intervention Board, PO Box 69, Reading RG1 3YD. Tel: (01189) 531141.

HM LAND REGISTRY

HM Land Registry has 20 regional offices located throughout England and Wales, each having devolved responsibility for the procurement of a broad range of goods and services.

Locating required goods and services

- postal services
- office machinery
- office consumables
- carrier services
- furniture
- fixtures and fittings.
- vehicles
- consultancy services

Accessing the route

Contracts are placed by competitive tendering and *many of these are suitable for small business.*

General procurement
Purchasing and Supply Unit, Room 017, HM Land Registry, Lincoln's Inn Field, London WC2A 3PH.

Information technology
IT Procurement Manager, HM Land Registry, Computer Services Division, Drakes Hill Court, Burrington Way, Plymouth PL5 3LP.

DEPARTMENT OF NATIONAL HERITAGE

This department has already outsourced the majority of its central support services, including information technology. Purchases of other goods are therefore limited to the relatively modest needs of the core department. *Good opportunities here nevertheless for small business operators.*

Accessing the route
Write in the first instance to: Department of National Heritage, Central Services Division, 2/4 Cockspur Street, London SW1Y 5DH.

METROPOLITAN POLICE SERVICE

The Metropolitan Police Service offers scope for firms of all sizes to enter the tendering process for the goods and services it requires.
Annual purchasing budget: £397 million.

Accessing the route
Contact: Assistant Director of Finance (Purchasing), Metropolitan Police Service, Cobalt Square, 1 South Lambeth Road, London SW8 1SU.

DEPARTMENT FOR NATIONAL SAVINGS

National Savings comprises a small headquarters and marketing operation together with three regionally based operating divisions, each of which has delegated purchasing responsibility.
HQ: London; Operating Divisions: Blackpool, Glasgow, Durham.

Locating goods and services
- furniture
- maintenance
- security services
- information technology
- software
- consumables.
- stationery
- printing

Accessing the route
National Savings places a substantial number of small value orders and as a result *there are considerable opportunities for small suppliers to meet these requirements.*
Contact: Procurement Unit, Department for National Savings, Charles House, 375 Kensington High Street, London W14 8SD. Tel: (020) 7605 9369.

Ask for a copy of *Suppliers' Guide for Selling to National Savings* which you will find useful.

NATURAL ENVIRONMENT RESEARCH COUNCIL

This department covers research in a wide variety of scientific disciplines.

Locating required goods and services
- office machinery
- stationery
- furniture
- scientific equipment
- cleaning
- security
- scientific supplies
- plant maintenance
- catering
- capital equipment
- machinery maintenance
- IT equipment.

Accessing the route
Procurement is undertaken by competitive tendering and your enquiry regarding procurement procedures should be addressed to: Chief Purchasing Officer, Natural Environment Research Council, Polaris House, North Star Avenue, Swindon SN2 1EU.

THE OFFICE FOR NATIONAL STATISTICS

This new agency provides a comprehensive range of official statistics and information on economy, society, business, population, the labour market, regions and health.

Locating required goods and services
- information technology
- consumables
- office services
- software
- office machinery
- stationery

- printing
- statistical surveys
- consultancy services.

Accessing the route
Write to: Procurement Unit, Office for National Statistics, Government Buildings, Cardiff Road, Newport, Gwent NP9 1XG. Tel: (01633) 812689. Fax: (01633) 813358.

OFFICE OF WATER SERVICES (OFWAT)

Many of this department's orders are of modest value and there are consequently *opportunities for small suppliers to meet the undernoted requirements.*

Locating required goods and services
- office cleaning
- printing
- business travel
- furniture
- office machinery
- courier services
- stationery
- information technology
- consultancy services.

Accessing the route
Contact: Office of Water Services, Centre City Tower, 7 Hill Street, Birmingham B5 4UA. Tel: (0121) 625 1347.

ORDNANCE SURVEY

Ordnance Survey buys a variety of goods, materials and services ranging from general office and IT equipment to specialist surveying and map production items.

Accessing the route
Contact the undernoted who will on request provide you with a copy of *Ordnance Survey – Suppliers' Guide.*
Procurement and Supplies Division, Ordnance Survey, Romsey Road, Southampton SO16 4GU.

OVERSEAS DEVELOPMENT ADMINISTRATION (ODA)

The ODA finances substantial purchases of goods and associated services (for the benefit of developing countries) in all fields except military equipment, luxury goods or tobacco related products.

Accessing the route
Procurement is normally undertaken by ODA registered agents to whom you should address your initial enquiries.
Crown Agents: St Nicholas House, St Nicholas Road, Sutton SM1 1EL. Tel: (020) 8643 3311 Fax (020) 8643 8232.
Balfour Williamson: Roman House, Wood Street, London EC2 5BP.
Regent Export plc: 6 Castle Street, Salisbury SP1 1BB. Tel: (01722) 338282. Fax: (01722) 327747.
MKT (Systems) Ltd: International House, 174 Three Bridges Road, Crawley, West Sussex RH10 1LE. Tel: (01293) 514263. Fax: (01293) 560968.
Further information: Assistant Purchasing Adviser, The Procurement Advisory & Monitoring Unit (PAMU), Overseas Development Administration, 94 Victoria Street, London SW1E 5JL. Tel: (020) 7917 0773.

UK PASSPORT AGENCY

The Passport Agency is responsible for the issuing of passports and visas and provides other related services for British Nationals in the United Kingdom.

Locating required goods and services
- stationery
- office machinery
- office supplies
- information technology
- software
- consumables
- furniture
- security printing
- career wear.

Accessing the route
Contact: United Kingdom Passport Agency, Procurement Unit, Clive House, 70/78 Petty France, London SW1H 9HD.

PUBLIC RECORD OFFICE (PRO)

The PRO buys various goods and services through a delegated purchasing system.

Locating required goods and services
- stationery
- furniture
- office equipment
- office supplies
- conservation equipment
- reprographic equipment
- consumables.

Accessing the route
Contact: Senior Purchasing Officer, Public Record Office, Ruskin Avenue, Kew, Surrey TW9 4DU.

ROYAL MINT

The Royal Mint is essentially a small factory and as such requires many specialist products. There is a *good opportunity here for little firms* but when tendering you should bear in mind that a particularly high standard of work is required by the Royal Mint.

Locating required goods and services
- precious metals
- base metals
- packaging.
- machinery
- tools
- scientific equipment
- chemicals

Accessing the route
Apply in writing to: The Purchasing Manager, The Royal Mint, Llantrisant, Pontyclun, Mid Glamorgan CF72 8YT. Alternatively telephone either Nigel Thomas or Trevor Pritchard on (01443) 222111.

ENGINEERING AND PHYSICAL SCIENCES RESEARCH COUNCIL (EPSRC)

There are a number of opportunities here for small business.

Locating required goods and services
- information technology
- consumables
- office furniture
- hardware
- consultancy services
- stationery
- software

Accessing the route
Apply in writing to: The Head of Procurement, EPSRC, Polaris House, North Star Avenue, Swindon SN2 1ET.

DEPARTMENT OF SOCIAL SECURITY (DSS)

A network of business units throughout the department undertakes procurement for the DSS. Each unit has a lead role in a particular area. The Director of Procurement and his team head up this network.

Accessing the route
In the first instance write to: Director of Procurement, Department of Social Security, Ground Floor East, 1 Trevelyan Square, Boar Lane, Leeds LS1 6EB.

Other useful addresses
DSS Executive Agencies: Vendor Management, GZ2 Government Buildings, Moorland Road, St Annes FY8 3ZZ. Tel: (01253) 334392.
Child Support Agency (CSA): Dudley CSA Centre, Quay House, The Waterfront, Level Street, Brierley Hill, West Midlands DY5 1XA. Tel: (01384) 574800.
Contributions Agency (CA): Contracts Services, Room 143b, Central Office DSS, Newcastle Upon Tyne NE98 1YX. Tel: (0191) 225 5943/225 3360.
Benefits Agency (BA): Ground Floor, 1 Trevelyan Square, Boar Lane, Leeds LS1 6EB. Tel: (0113) 232 7222..
War Pensions Agency (WPA): Room 6304, Norcross, Blackpool FY5 3WP. Tel: (01253) 333056.

DEPARTMENT OF TRADE AND INDUSTRY (DTI)

By and large, DTI operates a devolved budgeting system which delegates purchasing authority to managers so that they can buy direct from suppliers. However, at headquarters a number of goods and services are purchased centrally or through centrally let call-off arrangements.

Accessing the route
Contacts for centrally managed goods and services:
Building services: Department of Trade & Industry, 151 Buckingham Palace Road, London SW1W 9SS. Tel: (020) 7215 1269.

IT goods and services: Department of Trade & Industry, 151 Buckingham Palace Road, London SW1W 9SS. Tel: (020) 7215 3760. Publications: Information Directorate, 7.G.25, Department of Trade & Industry, 1/19 Victoria Street, London SW1 0ET. Tel: (020) 7215 5072.

For other goods and services in headquarters, information will be passed on to potential users and enquiries should in the first instance be addressed to:

Procurement Standards Unit, Department of Trade & Industry, 3.E.22, 1 Victoria Street, London SW1H 0ET. Tel: (020) 7215 5743.

If you are interested in supplying the executive agencies you should contact:

Companies House: Room 1.79, Companies House, Crown Way, Cardiff CF4 3UZ Tel: (029) 2038 0313. Fax: (029) 2038 0566.

Insolvency Service: Room 312, Insolvency Service, 21 Bloomsbury Street, London WC1B 3QW. Tel: (020) 7291 6756. Fax: (020) 7291 6764.

Patent Office: Patent Office, Room GB57, Concept House, Cardiff Road, Newport NP9 1RH. Tel: (01633) 814839. Fax: (01633) 814874.

Radiocommunications Agency: Radiocommunications Agency, Wyndham House, 189 Marsh Wall, London E14 9SX. Tel: (020) 7211 0406. Fax: (020) 7211 0413.

DEPARTMENT OF TRANSPORT

This department and its seven executive agencies purchase a wide variety of goods, works and services.

Locating required goods and services
- works
- research
- consultancy
- information technology
- office equipment
- office furniture.
- telecommunications

Accessing the route

To begin, apply for a copy of *Selling to the Department of Transport* which provides contact details for the various goods, works and services purchased by the department and its executive agencies. Copies are available from: Departmental Procurement Unit, Department of Transport, D Floor, Ashdown House, Sedlescombe Road North, St Leonards-on-Sea TN37 7GA. Tel: (01424) 458484.

HM TREASURY

The Treasury has a central purchasing unit which is responsible for all the goods and services bought by the department.

Locating required goods and services
- stationery
- office furniture
- electricity
- office equipment
- information technology
- travel
- office supplies
- cleaning
- consultancies.

Accessing the route
If you are interested in working with the Treasury in the first instance contact: Tel: (020) 7270 1304 and/or fax: (020) 7270 1305.

THE TREASURY SOLICITOR

The Treasury Solicitor's department provides litigation and advisory services to other government departments. It purchases the usual range of office equipment and stationery together with information technology products. *Quotes are obtained for small purchases* and formal tender procedures are applied to larger procurements.

Accessing the route
Office equipment supplies: The Office Services Manager, The Treasury Solicitor's Department, Queen Anne's Chambers, 28 Broadway, London SW1H 9JS. Tel: (020) 7210 3082.
Information technology: The Information Systems Manager, The Treasury Solicitor's Department, 28 Broadway, London SW1H 9JS. Tel: (020) 7210 3085.

NORTHERN IRELAND

The Government Purchasing Agency is a specialist unit with responsibility for purchasing activity across Northern Ireland Civil Service Departments and the Northern Ireland Office.

Accessing the route

Apply to the undernoted for a copy of *Selling to the Public Sector in Northern Ireland*, a good guide for potential suppliers which lists both the purchasing areas and relevant contact details.

Government Purchasing Agency, Rosepark House, Upper Newtownards Road, Belfast BT4 3NR. Tel: (01232) 526495. Fax: (01232) 526564.

THE SCOTTISH OFFICE

The Scottish Office consists of five main departments together with a central services group to provide support. There are 30 purchasing divisions (some of which are specialist units) within the Scottish Office and its related bodies. The Purchasing and Supply Division provides various co-ordination services.

Locating required goods and services

- stationery
- printing
- advertising
- information technology
- laboratory equipment

- catering
- furniture
- equipment
- research facilities
- cleaning

- telecommunications
- maintenance
- consultancy
- training
- career wear.

Accessing the route

Your initial letter of enquiry should be accompanied by details of products/services, a brief resumé of company structure (size, number of employees, etc) and an indication of other government departments you may have supplied. You should also include any trade brochures (12 of each).

Write to: The Scottish Office (Business Enquiries), Purchasing and Supply Division, Room 33/4, James Craig Walk, Edinburgh EH1 3BA. Tel: (0131) 244 3518. Fax: (0131) 244 3661.

THE WELSH OFFICE

To facilitate its administrative functions, the Welsh Office purchases goods and services valued at in excess of £20 million per annum.

Accessing the route

Enquiries regarding Welsh Office purchasing practices and those related to central goods and services should be addressed to:

Welsh Office, Procurement Unit, Cathays Park, Cardiff CF1 3NQ. Tel: (029) 2082 5665.

Companies who wish to be considered for inclusion in the tendering process for other goods and services should write to:

Roads: Welsh Office, Contracts Section, Roads Administration Division 1, Cathays Park, Cardiff CF1 3NQ.

Agriculture: Welsh Office, Agriculture Department, Purchasing Unit, Government Buildings, Spar Road East, Llandrindod Wells, Powys LD1 5HA.

NATIONAL HEALTH SERVICE (NHS)

Procurement in the NHS is no longer centrally controlled and the workload is now split between these authorities:

NHS Supplies Authority

This organisation purchases a wide range of products and services for the NHS throughout England.

- medical and surgical equipment and consumables
- food, catering equipment and hotel services
- information technology products and services
- vehicles
- utilities including gas, coal, oil, electricity and water
- major medical equipment, eg scanners
- patient appliances including orthotics and prosthetics
- drugs and pharmaceutical products.

NHS Supplies also offers a wide range of other services to hospitals and trusts including:

- handling day-to-day issues such as ordering and replenishing stock
- delivering goods and providing information on consumption, performance and value for money
- materials management – maintaining optimum ward and department stock levels
- consultancy services: capital equipping, market testing, public sector procurement procedures
- guiding customers through purchasing projects
- sale or disposal of second-hand equipment.

Accessing the route

If you are interested in finding out more about working with NHS Supplies, make contact with:

Managing Director – Purchasing, NHS Supplies, Apex Plazza, Forbury Road, Reading RG1 1AX. Tel: (0118) 959 5085. Fax: (0118) 956 7667.

Scottish Healthcare Supplies

There is a two-tier level for NHS procurement in Scotland with Scottish Healthcare Supplies (SHS) at the centre providing services which complement local supplies at each NHS Trust and Health Board.

* Trust Supplies Arrangements
* Scottish Healthcare Supplies.

Annual purchasing budget: £450 million.

Accessing the route

Potential suppliers should make application in writing to:

The Director, Scottish Healthcare Supplies, Trinity Park House, South Trinity Road, Edinburgh EH5 3SH. Tel: (0131) 552 6255.

Welsh Health Common Services Authority (WHCSA)

Welsh Health Supplies (a business unit of WHCSA) has the remit to negotiate contracts for the NHS in Wales.

Locating goods and services

* foodstuffs and provisions
* surgical products
* information technology
* textiles
* drugs
* radiological equipment
* uniforms
* energy
* engineering
* medical products
* utilities.

Accessing the route

Write formally (enclosing complete background details) to:

Welsh Health Supplies, Crickhowell House, Pierhead Street, Capital Waterside, Cardiff CF1 5XT.

HIGHER EDUCATION INSTITUTIONS

The Committee of Vice-Chancellors and Principals (CVCP) operates a Central Purchasing office which has produced a purchasing directory to provide present and potential suppliers with a clearer insight into how the sector's purchasing interests are organised and how they might be approached to best effect.

Annual purchasing budget: £2 billion.

Locating required goods and services
- audit services
- catering services
- legal services
- biochemicals
- office supplies
- maintenance
- vehicles
- stationery
- telecommunications
- janitorial services
- health and safety equipment
- laboratory supplies
- gases
- capital projects and equipment
- insurance
- energy
- building materials and services
- catering supplies
- information technology.

Accessing the route
Copies of the Purchasing Directory may be obtained from:
CVCP Office: 29 Tavistock Square, London, WC1H 9SZ. Tel: (020) 7387 9231. Fax: (020) 7388 8649.
CVCP Central Purchasing Co-ordinator (CPC), 34 Buccleuch Place, Edinburgh EH8 9JT. Tel: (0131) 650 4081. Fax: (0131) 667 9801.

Suppliers wishing to develop purchasing arrangements and agreements for the sector should contact: CVCP Assistant Central Purchasing Co-ordinator, Sheffield Hallam University, Pond Street, Sheffield S1 1WB. Tel: (0114) 253 3815. Fax: (0114) 253 3932.

Key regional contacts

North West: Regional Purchasing Co-ordinator, North Western Universities Purchasing Consortium (NWUPC), University of Liverpool, PO Box 147, Liverpool L69 3BX. Tel: (0151) 794 3130. Fax: (0151) 794 3133.

North East: Group Purchasing Co-ordinator, North Eastern Universities Purchasing Group (NEUPG), NEUPG Office, 156 Broomspring Lane, Sheffield S10 2FE. Tel: (0114) 275 2420. Fax: (0114) 275 2420.

South: Southern Universities Purchasing Consortium (SUPC), The University of Reading, London Road, Reading RG1 5AQ. Tel: (0118) 931 6542. Fax: (0118) 931 6404.

London: Director, London Universities Purchasing Consortium (LUPC), Mackenzie House, Millman Mews, Millman Street, London WC1N 3EH. Tel: (020) 7405 8400. Fax: (020) 7430 1266.

Midlands: Co-ordinator, Midlands Universities Purchasing Consortium (MUPC), Coventry University, Priory Street, Coventry CV1 5FB. Tel: (0120) 383 8767. Fax: (0120) 383 8995.

Scotland and Northern Ireland: Secretary, Joint Consultative & Advisory Committee on Purchasing, 34 Buccleuch Street, Edinburgh EH8 9JT. Tel: (0131) 650 4080. Fax: (0131) 667 9801.

Wales: Purchasing Co-ordinator, Higher Education Purchasing Consortium Wales (HEPCW), University of Wales, University Registry, Cathays Park, Cardiff CF1 3NS. Tel: (029) 2038 2656. Fax: (029) 2039 6040.

LOCAL AUTHORITIES

Collectively, local authorities have enormous purchasing power and buy a huge range of goods and services. They make their own decisions on the way they invite tenders and in awarding contracts take stringent cognisance of both EC procurement rules and UK legislation which includes compulsory competitive tendering (CCT).

CCT applies to a broad spectrum of local authority work and services which means that an authority can only carry out certain defined activities in-house if the work has first gone out to tender and been won in open competition.

The purchasing organisation within authorities varies from one to another but here are the four basic approaches you will encounter:

1. Authorities which permit each potential unit to buy for itself.

2. Authorities where the unit which buys most acts for all the others.

3. Authorities which have a central purchasing facility providing for all units.

4. Authorities where goods and services are bought through a consortium.

The biggest consortia are concerned exclusively with purchasing and distribution for their member authorities. There are others though which specialise in buying particular product ranges.

Accessing the route

There are various types of local authorities and there are various ways of approaching them. You could refer to the telephone directory or *Yellow Pages* for details of those councils of interest to you and contact them direct for information on their purchasing methods and requirements. Alternatively (and a much better bet) is to obtain a copy of the *Municipal Yearbook and Public Services Directory* which lists the major consortia and provides contact points in councils throughout the United Kingdom. Copies are available from:

Book Sales Department, Newman Books, 32 Vauxhall Bridge Road, London SW1V 2SS. Tel: (020) 7973 6400.

Individual enquiries on local authority tendering issues should be addressed to:

Local Government Competition and Quality Division, Department of the Environment, 5th Floor, Erland House, Bressendon Place, London SW1E 5DU. Tel: (020) 7890 4145.

You have now examined many proven strategies and accessed the routes to doing business in the public sector. In Part 3 we look at ways of perfecting the techniques essential to selling successfully in this exciting multi-billion pound marketplace.

7

Marketing Your Product or Service

The way you go about marketing your product or service to the public sector in the early days is crucial. The image you create at the outset is likely to be the one that will stick with you right through all your dealings. All the more reason then to get it right, at the start.

So much nonsense is talked about marketing, when the essence of good marketing is no more than the application of sound common sense.

Marketing is communication, *effective communication*, in absolutely everything connected with the process which leads to the point where the customer decides to buy (or not to buy).

WHAT MARKETING IS NOT

To elaborate on the much abused term 'marketing', communication is the essence of all business. The 'best talkers' are not necessarily those who communicate best, it depends how you project your unique personality, how you articulate, how you relate to people without using words at all, how you listen.

Marketing is *not* advertising promotions, public relations, exhibitions, premiums, grand openings, closing down sales and the like. It certainly includes all these but a great deal more besides.

Marketing is a common sense approach to conducting business. It involves how you dress, speak, relate to your customers, treat your staff, set up your stall – what kind of image you create for yourself and your enterprise.

Where do we make a start with all this? Right here, right now, with you.

PROJECTING THE ESSENTIAL YOU

You're all you've got, so make the most of yourself. It's the *essential you* that must come across when you start dealing with officials in the public sector. They have an innate distrust of people who evidence 'side' in their negotiations. There must be no side to you. Be

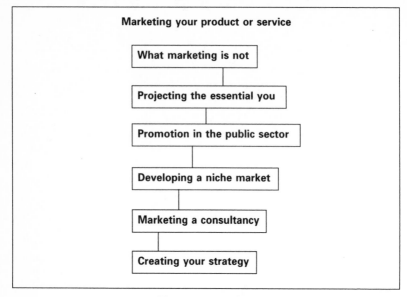

Fig. 8. Marketing.

yourself at all times and you'll rapidly begin to build up trust with your opposite numbers in the public sector marketplace.

Don't even think about changing because you couldn't if you tried. Changing you is not on the agenda. Concentrate rather on who you are, what you are and why you are.

When you move on in time to hustle your stuff in the other big marketplace in the sky, it won't be your goods or services people down here will remember you by, it will be the essential you that sticks in the memory.

- dress well
- speak well
- walk well
- be calm
- be courteous
- be truthful
- be a good listener
- project well
- earn (but never command) respect.

Projecting the essential you is the first and most important piece of marketing you'll ever undertake in your quest for success in the public sector marketplace.

HOW TO PROMOTE IN THE PUBLIC SECTOR

The good news is, it won't cost much, and whatever you budget should be expended on selective below-the-line promotional activities. Full-page full colour ads won't get you on the tender list, but careful attention to well reasoned, strategic marketing will help to get you there.

Polish up your presentation skills

This is an area of prime importance in promoting your service to the public sector. You know your business inside out but unless you can explain and demonstrate your expertise easily and effortlessly to your audience, your words will fall on deaf ears.

If personal presentation is a weak spot in your repertoire, polish up your act now before taking it out on the road . . .

Working with existing print matter

There is no requirement on you to produce a special range of print matter in promoting to public sector officials. Only invest in this if you hit upon a niche aspect to your product or service which you feel needs additional or exclusive exposure. All you'll normally be asked to submit prior to being invited to tender is a selection of current literature together with an up-to-date price list.

Do not in any event bombard officials with targeted fliers because if you do, they'll land straight in the bin.

Budget for some trade advertising

Subscribe to and read 'trade' journals such as *Government Opportunities, MoD Contracts Bulletin, Local Government Chronicle* etc. Apart from any other consideration they carry invitation-to-tender notices, but also on occasion you'll get prior warning of special supplements within certain of which it may prove advantageous for you to place one-off advertisements.

Using PR selectively and effectively

Once again, look for opportunities to use the trade press, but this time for free. If you've just won a public sector contract, tell them; if you've been invited to tender, tell them; if you've recently added a new dimension to your service which may be of interest, tell them. Selective press relations in public sector journals is an excellent and free way of getting your name and service circulating in the right market areas.

Don't employ anyone else to do it for you. Do it yourself. It's simple and it's a good discipline for you to develop.

Attend public sector seminars and conferences

Make a point of sourcing information on forthcoming public sector seminars and conferences within striking distance of your locale (the journal relevant to your field of activity will carry this data) and choose the most appropriate one. Sometimes you can get in free, sometimes you have to pay. Whatever, visit the venues of your choice. It's a great way to make vital contacts and bone up on news that may be critical to your aspirations.

Develop your image at exhibitions

Both central and local government host exhibitions throughout the United Kingdom at regular intervals. Find the one(s) best suited to you and if you can afford it, rent a small stand. I can vouch for the fact that not only will you make valuable contacts, you might also do substantial business.

If you can't afford a stand, take a day trip and put yourself around among the public sector exhibitors.

DEVELOPING A NICHE MARKET

Sometimes, maybe not often, you can spot an opening where, with a little fine tuning, your product or service fits neatly into a surprising and unexpected niche in the market.

This happened to me in the area of specialist sponsored publishing (covered earlier). The opening located was tailor-made for the publishing arm of the marketing consultancy, and within no more than 18 months contracts were obtained and production completed for the following full-colour local authority publications. Some of these titles struggled to attract advertising revenue and barely broke even; others prospered and returned handsome dividends: *Clydebank Official Guide*; *Gateshead Environmental Handbook*; *Hamilton Business Directory*; *Sedgefield District Guide & Map*; *South Tyneside Planning Handbook*; *Hartlepool Environmental Services Annual Review*; *London Borough of Camden Guide*; *Malvern Hills Environmental Handbook*; *South Wales Business Directory*; *Dundee Enterprise Trust Directory*; *Gloucester City Guide to Environmental Services*.

Look closely at your product or service and see if you can discover an aspect that you could develop, and then niche market in the public sector.

Observe the diversity of local authority areas in the list of publications. You can sell anywhere in the public sector if you're good enough.

Footnote: a totally unscheduled bonus came the way of the consultancy as a direct result of the niche activity described. On public sector recommendation, the publishing arm was awarded a major private sector contract: the design and production of a 400pp user manual for a multi-national electronics firm with worldwide distribution.

MARKETING A CONSULTANCY SERVICE

As a marketing services consultant of long standing I can talk with some authority on marketing consultancy services in the public sector. The opportunities are abundant for practitioners in almost every field of management consultancy and these opportunities fall broadly into the same areas as they would if you were selling a range of merchandise.

- central government departments
- local authorities
- executive agencies
- NHS hospitals and trusts
- other public bodies (police, fire, national parks, etc).

Sourcing assignments

You will find yourself working a little harder than the average purveyor of hard tack goods. The reason for this is not just competition from your peers, but chiefly because public sector officials tend to use a wide net in their selection process for appointing appropriate consultants. They are very much into 'match and match' (matching specific projects to specific specialists).

As most consultancy projects in the public sector are put out to tender, the process can often be long drawn out and involve participants in a deal of expense (briefings, research, presentations, more meetings). It is not unusual in phase one for a department to invite as many as a dozen firms to pitch for the work, and in phase two to short-list three to six as tenderers.

ITTs (**invitations to tender**) are frequently and automatically extended to established and larger practices, leaving new entrants to the public sector market to forage harder for openings.

Despair not though, there's still plenty to go around, no matter your speciality. Consultancies from the largest to the smallest operate consistently and successfully in the public sector. Many of these are sole traders specialising in a particular vein of expertise.

What you have to do as a new entrant is to set about the task of . . .

Marketing yourself
You'll accomplish this best by implementing and adhering to these directives.

1. Project the essential you.
2. Stick to what you specialise in.
3. Identify your specific markets.
4. Target them through consistent research.
5. Cultivate contacts within your prescribed markets.
6. Look out for invitations to tender.
7. Don't wait to be asked though, be proactive.
8. Use selective PR to put your name and service around.
9. Perfect your presentation skills.

Make all of this your code of practice and you will prosper in the public sector.

What are the differences?
Are there any major differences to be considered when consulting in the public sector? Not really, apart from those associated with the precautionary policies and procedures employed by those responsible for purchasing out of the public purse. Accountability is all and (as with goods and general services) value for money is germane to awarding contracts for consultancy services.

By and large the public sector is becoming market conscious and therefore commercially minded in transacting business with the private sector.

Why are there so many consultancy opportunities?
The demand on the public sector for the adoption of a more commercially oriented approach (and accordingly an increasing demand for consultancy services) has been occasioned in the main by:

- Resource accounting. An initiative to create an accounting and budgeting system similar to that used in the private sector.

- The Citizen's Charter. Launched to raise the standard of public services and make them more responsive to the needs of end users.

- The Next Steps Programme. The creation of the executive agencies to assist government in the execution of its responsibilities.

- Compulsory competitive tendering (CCT). The measure designed to ensure balance all round in the competitive tendering process.

- Marketing testing of services. Testing the value for money offered by in-house services through competitive tendering involving private sector suppliers.

- Privatisation initiatives. The incidence of privatising public utilities.

What does the future hold?
The market is booming and will continue to do so for as long as consultancies not only offer, but also demonstrate, value for money in their projects and recommendations.

DRAWING UP YOUR STRATEGY

Drawing up an effective marketing strategy in the early stages is the key to success in the long run. Keep it short, crisp, even, and if you can contain it to a single sheet of A4, so much the better. That way you'll remember it and employ it automatically in all your dealings.

Whatever else has to be implemented in the light of your particular operation, your strategy should also include:

1. A commitment to projecting the essential you.
2. Your initial promotional plans.
3. An appraisal of niche marketing potential.

CASE STUDY

The Greystroke Marketing Partnership was having a bumpy ride at the first briefing meeting on its pitch to tender for an important piece of local authority business. Bob blamed his partner Brian for the shambles and told him so on their return to the office.

'I'm sorry now I allowed myself to be persuaded to let you handle today's presentation. It was nothing short of appalling.'

'Appalling? You've got some nerve . . .' countered Brian testily.

'No, you're the one with the nerve. What about all that guff you gave them regarding focus groups? Pre-testing everything in advance before we do it for our clients. You know we've never done that. Maybe we should, but the fact is we never have.'

'Yeah, well, they're not to know that.'

'They soon will if you ask around our clients. You gave them a list, don't forget.'

'You're over-reacting.'

'Correction. You were *overacting*. Now, let's see if we can salvage something out of all this before the next meeting. Let's examine who we are at Greystroke, what we are, why we are, and then rebuild our presentation from that.'

EXERCISE

The personal plan of action you started as an exercise in Chapter 1 has gathered momentum. Bring it up to speed in the light of what you've learned to date.

8

Adding Power to Your Negotiations

Do you know someone who never takes 'no' for an answer, who always bounces back, often unexpectedly and with increased enthusiasm for the task on hand, or someone who always seems able to circumvent problems in an inventive way?

Then you know someone who knows something about effective negotiation.

To the uninitiated, such people may on occasion come across as a pain in the neck but the fact is they understand the basic tenets of the negotiation process. This is not to suggest that when you master the art of negotiation you too will be in danger of becoming an irritation to others. On the contrary, you will find yourself dealing competently and confidently with all your affairs and developing an ability to treat quantifiable success and apparent failure with equanimity. You will look upon the results of your deliberations as 'outcomes' rather than successes or failures, and in the process add power to your negotiations.

For too long, too few have jealously guarded the 'secrets' surrounding something that is no more than myth. The myth is that the tactics of effective negotiations are shrouded in mystique.

The secret is ... there are no secrets.

LEARNING THE BASICS

Learn to *communicate* efficiently, and you will learn to *negotiate* effectively. It's as simple as that, it's a matter of applied common sense. However, to accelerate the learning curve, you will do well to acquire a firm grasp on the principles, guidelines and signposts that form the core of this chapter.

The essential key to effective negotiation
Make it your goal always to achieve a **win-win** result in all your transactions. Win-win is good – for you and for the other party – and especially so (*crucial* even) in the case of public sector negotiation. Never allow an impasse to strangle your negotiations. Always ensure that

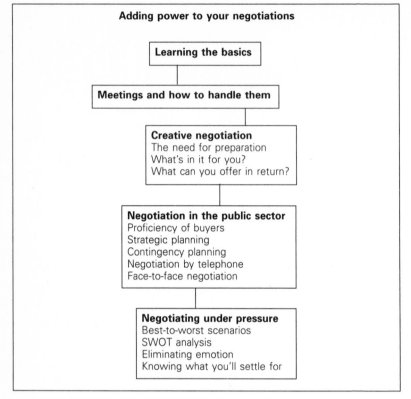

Fig. 9. The power of effective negotiation.

there is something left for you and the other person to hang onto, something to hope for in the final outcome.

When the win-win approach is absent from negotiation, both parties will want what *they* want and be incapable of seeing how they can attain it without crushing the other person's aspirations.

Many potential tenderers find their negotiations floundering at an early stage. Lack of understanding is usually the reason. Because they don't understand the art of effective negotiation, fear sets in; and because they haven't yet mastered the essential procedures for selling in the public sector, fear takes control.

But what is there to fear? Negotiation and selling go hand in hand. Master the techniques and there's nothing to fear. Even in the most difficult of negotiation circumstances, there's always something you can give. It might be as painless as a softening of attitude, an undertaking to show willing to engage in further discussion. Adopt the win-

win approach from the outset of your public sector adventure. You'll need it to survive and prosper.

- Win-win is good for both parties.
- Never walk away in a huff.
- You only take out of negotiation what you put into it yourself.
- Always leave the other person with their dignity intact.
- Demand what you want and you'll get what you deserve.

MEETINGS AND HOW TO HANDLE THEM

Before you engage in any meeting with anyone, on any matter at any time, ask yourself the following:

1. Who called this meeting?

2. Why?

3. What's on the agenda?

4. What's the *real* purpose of the meeting?

5. Who will be in attendance?

6. Why am I invited?

7. What will be expected of me?

8. Is there something I don't know about yet?

9. What's in it for me?

10. What's the best I could hope to achieve?

11. Would I settle for less if things don't go my way?

If you think the foregoing only applies in corporate commercial situations, think again. You will need to protect yourself through adequate preparation every bit as much in the public sector as you would in your private sector dealings.

The new breed of public sector buyer is commercially focused nowadays. You'll find yourself being called to all sorts of meetings with all sorts of people. Most of them will genuinely want to do business with you while others will just pick your brains for free if you let them.

Never allow yourself to be caught out unprepared. If you are at all unsure as to why you have been invited, ask in advance. Whether it's a major opportunity or a potential let down, better you know the facts before you attend so that you have time to prepare an appropriate strategy.

Beware of the hidden agenda
Should your prior investigations prove to be inconclusive and you are taken by surprise in the opening dialogue, simply respond, 'I wouldn't wish to comment on that. Provide me with some background on the issue and I'll gladly come back later and discuss the matter with you.'

CREATIVE NEGOTIATION PAYS OFF

Always endeavour to be creative in your negotiations and you can do this by making sufficient advance preparation, establishing in your own mind exactly what it is you want from the interface, and what you have to offer in return.

Win-win, remember?

The need for preparation
Some people walk into delicate negotiations brimming with angst or worse still, smarting from an unhealthy level of bile in the belly. They want to stand their corner, they want to speak their mind, they want to shout, they want to fight. Standing your corner and stating your case are fine, they're essential parts of the game plan. Raising your voice or becoming belligerent are taboo for the thinking negotiator who intends to make a positive mark in the public sector.

People who over-react (or overact) at meetings are the ones who arrive unprepared, uninformed and frequently unwilling to listen. Don't ever fall into this trap in a public sector group dialogue situation. Come prepared and you will make an immediate impression, the right impression.

- Always prepare in advance for impending negotiation.
- Don't walk into a meeting with a chip on your shoulder.

Establishing exactly what you want
This does not mean getting in first and laying it on the line for the others to digest and react accordingly. Do it that way and you'll get a reaction you don't want. It means defining in your preparations precisely what it is you want out of the negotiation and devising the method you will adopt to achieve your aims.

The method will invariably consist in *listening* intently to all other viewpoints, collating fresh intelligence along the way, balancing or adjusting your stance as required, and introducing your own (perhaps revised) viewpoint at an appropriate juncture when the others have exhausted theirs.

Effective negotiation is not unlike the game of brag. If you are in *control* then you only turn your cards face up when the other players have shown their hands.

- Don't jump in straightaway with your 'wants' list.
- Listen, observe and take note of other viewpoints.
- State your case when the others have presented theirs.

These are the techniques you must always employ when attending briefing meetings with public sector officials. Do it this way and they'll say when you leave, 'This guy really knows his stuff . . .'

Knowing what you have to offer in return

You may win hands down and get exactly what you want the first time of asking and without giving back anything in return. Again, you may not, and in that event you'd better have come prepared to bargain. Value is only what a person perceives it to be, and in win-win neither party loses out if they are both on the same wavelength.

However, if you haven't done your homework and the other party has, you may find yourself steamrollered into parting with more in return than you would prefer or can afford.

- Come prepared with something in return for what you want.
- Never give back what you can't afford.

WHY PREPARATION IS ESSENTIAL IN PUBLIC SECTOR NEGOTIATION

If you still need convincing on the need for painstaking preparation, then read the following extract from a document produced by the Central Unit of Procurement on key directives for effective negotiation. This document was not produced for the enhancement of your negotiation technique but for that of your opposite number, the public sector buyer.

Guidance for contracting strategic services

1. Obtain training if you are new to negotiating or seek assistance from experienced negotiators.

2. Plan and prepare negotiation strategies in advance.

3. Be clear about your aims, what you have to offer, what the supplier has to offer.

4. Determine the aims to be achieved.

5. Assess realistically what is of value to you and the other party.

6. Assess which party is under most time pressure.

7. Assess which party has most to lose if negotiations break down.

8. Review the process in order to learn for the future.

   ... and if you still need convincing...

Contingency Planning

1. Are the existing contingency plans adequate?

2. What would the authority do if the supplier were unable to deliver the required service?

3. Is accepting some delay feasible while sourcing a replacement supplier?

4. What are the plans for establishing emergency cover?

Remember, these directives on preparing for negotiation are for the benefit of the public sector buyer. If you want to be successful in your negotiations, you need to be on at least the same level of preparedness if you are to get past the first briefing meeting intact.

Something up your sleeve

Do your preparation for negotiation as prescribed but go one stage further if you anticipate that a particular meeting of minds could prove troublesome and require you to exercise subtle discretion in your submission.

Example

Let's take a hypothetical example and construct a strategy in advance to manage the situation.

- You are a sole trading painter and decorator.
- You've only been in business on your own for two years.
- Your cash flow is balancing on a knife edge.
- You're always on the lookout for new assignments.

Out of the blue you are invited to take over a public sector contract for which you tendered but weren't successful. You want the contract, you need the contract, but there's an alarm bell ringing in your head. You make some enquiries around the trade and are informed that the previous incumbent walked out on the job after only two weeks. Your source of intelligence declines to comment further on the situation. You are facing two choices. Attend the meeting or refuse the offer.

Here's what you do. Take a sheet of A4 and construct a strategy for the negotiation.

Throgmorton County Council Housing Repairs Contract

On the bright side	*On the downside*
1. It's a nice piece of business	If it's that nice, why did the other fellow walk out?
2. The timescale is okay	Is it? What if they've trimmed it because the job's behind schedule?
3. The money's good	How good now? If I have to do more in less time, will I make a profit?
4. It'll ease my cash flow	Will it? What if they pay late?

Conclusions

1. I've got some questions to ask these people at the County Council.

2. I'd better get assurances before accepting.

Action

1. Ask why the incumbent walked out on the job.

2. Get a firm time schedule out of them and adjust the price accordingly.

3. Ask for part payment in advance.

Option

If they won't come up with satisfactory answers, walk away.

Creative negotiation is all down to pre-planning and while our painter may or may not get the answers he's looking for, at worst he has prepared himself in advance for a potential letdown.

NEGOTIATING BY TELEPHONE

You will need to conduct some of your negotiations by telephone where both parties have to cope with two distinct disadvantages.

- You can't look into the other person's eyes.
- You can't observe the body language.

With practise, though, these drawbacks can be overcome by training yourself to listen out for varying tones and inflections in the voice of the person who's addressing you. Developing gradual competence in this technique is particularly useful when the telephone negotiation is being conducted with someone you have never met in person.

Some tell-tale voice signals

- Bluster: you've wrong-footed the other person.
- Sharp intake of breath: you may have caused unintentional offence or upset.
- Long pause: deliberation.
- Excessive chatter: attempting to bludgeon you into submission with pointless dialogue.
- Constant interruption: someone who doesn't want to know.
- Anxiety: unsure of facts.
- Abrupt end to conversation: you may have blown this one.

As video telecommunication increases, negotiating by telephone will take on a whole new dimension. However, it will never be exactly the same or as personal as face-to-face negotiation because of the distance factor.

Setting the parameters

The majority of telemarketers are trained to negotiate confidently and efficiently over the telephone and an essential part of their training is the **cue sheet**. It may be an electronic message on the VDU screen facing them or a lucidly composed script attached to a clipboard. You too should adopt this useful practice in preparation for your public sector telephone negotiations.

Before either making or receiving such foreseeable calls, jot down on a piece of paper all the factors which might have a bearing on the outcome of the conversation, prioritise them and highlight those of special significance (much as you would do for a face-to-face meeting). Should the negotiation appear likely to be more complex or problematic, then adopt the more comprehensive approach of our aforementioned painter and decorator: list the pros and cons, draw your conclusions, determine your anticipated action and decide on the options at your disposal.

- annotate
- prioritise
- highlight.

Failure to make adequate preparation will result in you being the party giving out tell-tale vocal signals.

Avoiding confrontation

Seems too obvious to mention, doesn't it? Yet people do it, over and over again, in telephone negotiation. They allow themselves to be goaded into faceless confrontation which rapidly turns into faceless acrimony, often souring an otherwise good working relationship. There are certain remarks you can make to a person *in person* which are unacceptable when written down (especially in an e-mail message) or made over the telephone. It's the missing eyes that cause the trouble, replaced in turn by misinterpretation and heightened umbrage.

Never enter into confrontation in your public sector negotiations. If you sense confrontation looming, back off. There's no win-win here, both parties lose out.

Follow up with a meeting if you are in doubt

On occasion when you are negotiating by telephone you will come across a scenario where almost everything on your checklist clicks into place with automatic precision. Yes, yes, yes; no 'nos' to sting your ears. You put down the receiver, review your list with glowing satisfaction, and then you begin to wonder.

'Does he really mean yes to *that* one? Was he paying attention? Why did he rush through everything? Does he understand what this contract's all about?'

Should this ever happen to you, ask for an early meeting.

There are people (even in the public sector) who are quite literally 'yes' people. They'll say yes to almost anything to get you off their list so that they can move on to the next piece of nonsense. It's all a bit of a game to them but it could be a case of survival for you. Meet with the other party, clarify everything agreed verbally, and then request that it all be confirmed in writing. If you don't you may find that they've moved on by the time you come to submit your invoice.

- Ask for a meeting if in doubt.
- Clarify the validity of all verbal affirmations.

OBSERVING SIGNS IN FACE-T0-FACE NEGOTIATION

Learn the significance of body language (earlobe tugging, nose scratching, sideways glances and the like) but don't be tempted to put too much store in any of this. Some people indulge in body language as a cover-up for their basic insecurities, others are just plain fidgety, some are simply having you on. Concentrate rather on linking meaningful body language to buying signals (when the eyes light up suddenly, for example).

Some prospects can't help giving away their intentions in this way – but for the rest, treat it with a degree of scepticism.

Developing an eyeball strategy

In meetings you have the advantage of eyeball-to-eyeball interface. If you already know the people you will have a fair idea of what to expect in the way of physical reactions during the course of the discussion. If you don't know them, quietly observe the *meaningful* body language for a few minutes, and you will get an early indication as to how they generally conduct themselves at meetings:

- prepare
- listen
- take note
- discuss
- ask.

Removing contention

Always be on the lookout for the token dissenter in your public sector group discussions. There's usually one in attendance. They tend to make their presence felt early on in discussion. Don't be fazed and avoid contentious reaction. Allow the dissenter to score a few harmless points but, if the conversation is in danger of being stifled, field the remarks with authority and calm professional expertise. Dissenters are prone to retreat when their wings are quietly but effectively clipped.

- Allow dissenters to noise off.
- React with calm, dignity and professional aplomb.

NEGOTIATING UNDER PRESSURE

It is a near certainty that sometime or another you will be obliged to engage in public sector negotiation under pressure, sometimes extreme pressure. These **pressurised negotiations** will arise in various circumstances (project falling behind schedule, materials failing to turn up in time, unscheduled changes in direction, etc) but if you can harness the pressure, you can turn it to your advantage.

Dissecting the issue
Whatever the issue, you must dissect the core of it before commencing your pressurised negotiations. Few situations are so extreme as to be irreversible and few causes are so far down the line as to be completely lost.

Devising best-to-worst scenarios
Take the bones of your investigation and do a SWOT analysis (examining the strengths, weaknesses, opportunities and threats). Sift out the strengths (however fragile), the weaknesses (however daunting), the opportunities (however slim) and the immediate threats. Devise several probable scenarios ranging from **best to worst**. Be pragmatic about this and don't cling on to any one particular scenario. Just put them all to the back of your mind until you engage in your pressure pot negotiations. Do this and you will discover that reason takes command when you get down to brass tacks on the vexing matter confronting you.

- Investigate all aspects of the problem.
- Do a SWOT analysis.
- Devise best-to-worst scenarios.
- Keep an open mind on the alternatives.

Eliminating emotion from your negotiations
You've examined the problem in all its shades of hope and despair, you've analysed them, you've prepared yourself for every eventuality. Now do one more thing, leave emotion out of your negotiations. You're pressurised enough as it is.

Knowing what you'll settle for
This is the bottom line in all negotiations conducted under pressure. You must always know in advance of the outcome exactly what you

are prepared to settle for in each of the scenarios you have devised. It helps take some of the sting out of the final reality.

CASE STUDY

The floor had given way on Concept Carpeting, or so it seemed to its sales director, Rob. He called his colleague, the managing director, from the council offices. 'The procurement officer is fuming, He won't wear any delay, he doesn't want to know, and he's threatening us with cancellation of the contract.'

Concept had won the tender to carpet the council offices throughout and this was the biggest piece of business they'd had for years. The problem now facing them was non-arrival of the required materials from Concept's main supplier.

'It's the end of the road for us,' lamented Rob. 'We'll never get another public sector contract after this. I don't know why I bother . . .'

'Calm down Rob,' soothed the MD. 'Get back here as fast as you can – but before you leave, fix up another meeting for tomorrow morning.'

'What good will that do?'

'When you get back we'll sit down and engage in some crisis management on this one. We'll find a way around the debacle. There's always a way and we'll find it between us.'

EXERCISE

You are faced with a problem similar to Rob's. Relate it to your own business and come up with a strategy for conducting negotiations (under pressure) on damage limitation.

9

Perfecting your Sales Technique

- *When you've learned to communicate, you've learned to negotiate, and you've also learned how to sell.*

Proficiency in communication and negotiation makes for good salesmanship. However, you're not quite there yet. There are a few more ground rules to become acquainted with before you go out into the public sector marketplace to sell your output with professional expertise.

When you have perfected your sales technique, you will have acquired complete mastery over the procedures essential for selling successfully and consistently to the public sector.

HOW TO BEGIN

You begin by taking stock of your current technique. Is it direct, forthright, outspoken, or do you adopt a more studied approach? Whatever, review it in the light of what you've learned so far from this book about selling procedures in the public sector, because by the time you've finished reading this chapter you will perhaps need to adjust your stance somewhat.

If you have little or no experience of face-to-face selling (maybe you've always had someone else around to do it for you), take heart. You may find it hard to acquire the selling habit to start with, but after a while you'll get hooked on it. All you've done so far is set up your stall; now you're on the biggest learning curve of your life. Even if you've been in sales all your career, you'll still be starting at square one because this time it's *all* down to you.

If your career path has been in a different direction altogether, or you've never sold face-to-face before, how are you going to master the art in a short time? Whether you realise it or not, you've been selling face-to-face since the day you were born; every time you screamed for attention in your cot, asked for extra pocket money, asked the boss for a raise or talked your way out of trouble, you were selling.

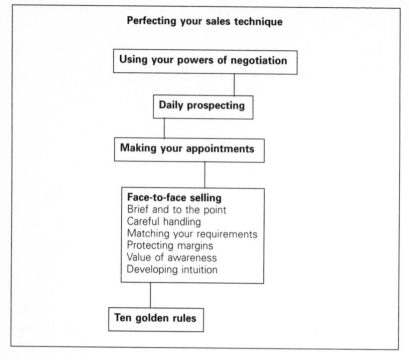

Fig. 10. Sales technique.

- Take stock of your sales technique.
- Review it in the light of your knowledge of selling procedures in the public sector.
- Make adjustments as required.

USING YOUR POWERS OF NEGOTIATION

Your ability to negotiate effectively will be the cornerstone of your (revised) sales technique. Note the emphasis placed by the public sector on training buyers in the art of effective negotiation and understand fully why this investment is made. Selling to government is all down to negotiation because there are no quick fixes, no loss leaders, no seconds or sub-standards, no bargain buys, no special offers – only value for money in every transaction – and establishing the principles therein takes time, patience and discussion.

You'll never actually *sell* anything to the public sector but they will *buy* from you if you take the trouble to identify their needs and satisfy them accordingly.

- Recognise that you are dealing with trained negotiators.
- Understand the concept of value for money.
- Realise the need for patience.

PROSPECTING FOR OPPORTUNITIES

We have already covered the myriad of methods available to you in your quest for opportunities to tender for projects and win contracts. Prospecting for opportunities isn't something you try your hand at now and again when there's nothing more interesting to do with your time. It must be a daily routine, a fixed entry in your diary, because without it you will very quickly have nowhere to go to pick up public sector business.

- Take some time out every day for prospecting.
- Look at every available avenue.
- Keep your opportunities database up to date.

MAKING YOUR APPOINTMENTS

Always use the telephone to make the appointment, not to make a sale. It doesn't work that way in the public sector. Try selling to them on the phone and you'll get short shrift. They might just *buy* from you by telephone occasionally when you're dealing with local purchases (where no contract is required) and they're desperate for your stuff. Don't hold your breath though for calls on that one.

Attempting to sell over the telephone is a cardinal error that has resulted in many a company ending up on public sector black lists.

All the purchasing we've been talking about is of a **considered** nature and should be treated accordingly by potential vendors, even if the purchase in question is for half a dozen boxes of tissue paper.

- Make your appointments by telephone.
- Never try to sell that way.
- Treat all enquiries for goods and services as 'considered' purchases.

FACE-TO-FACE SELLING

When you're communicating efficiently, you are selling; when you're negotiating with expertise, you are selling; when you evidence mastery of the essential procedures, you are also selling. What are you selling? You're selling *you*, and when you sell *you*, you are selling your service. If you fail to sell *you*, you'll sell nothing at all. That's why it is so important to work on the essential you before engaging in face-to-face negotiation.

Brief and to the point

Listen, take note and state your case. Keep it brief, succinct and to the point. Avoid unnecessary embellishment. It's a good ploy at the outset of your pitch to invite questions at the end in order to eliminate unsettling interruptions midway through.

Handling the prospect with care

When you are negotiating to sell always exercise respect for the buying party's feelings. If they occasionally cut across your delivery, let them. If they get touchy now and then, let them. If they pull holes in your presentation, let them. Any or all of this may be down to their own insecurities. Stay composed and concentrate on getting that invitation to tender or the contract approved.

Regardless of their foibles, respect the prospect and the prospect will respect you.

Matching your own requirements.

Never 'buy' assignments in your public sector negotiations or you'll quickly go bust. Taking on business at break-even levels just to keep the cash rolling in is folly. You are selling your skills to make a living but you won't make a living if you don't make a profit on every transaction. Value for money is a laudable concept in the public sector – but not at your expense. Steel yourself to negotiate and sell for profit in everything you do and don't give out freebies.

- Never deal in break-even deals.
- No freebies.

Protecting your margins

It's a temptation in the early days to play around with gross **margins** to attract the sort of business you *really* want to work on. Take care when you engage in this practice, because if you should happen to land a sizeable public sector contract through this type of discounting, you may be obliged to work on reduced profit levels for evermore on *everything* you undertake for public sector clients. You will have negotiated yourself into downsizing your overall gross margins for the sake of gratifying your early whims.

- Discounts spell danger.
- Don't risk downsizing your overall gross profit.

The value of awareness
Cultivate your awareness in negotiating to sell. Look out for buying signals and keep in mind the fact that acute awareness is the stock-in-trade of the thinking negotiator.

Developing intuitive techniques
Master the art of listening intently and something magical will happen time and time again. Your intuition will lead you by the hand to the correct approach in all circumstances of your negotiations.

Don't be an eager beaver
Eager beavers ignore five core rules of effective negotiation:

1. They're too keen (and it shows).

2. They talk too much (unsettling the prospect).

3. They ignore buying signals (they can't see them).
4. They gloss over the benefits (going for an early kill).

5. They make mistakes in their presentation (they're unprepared).

   Adopt instead the laid back listening approach. Give your prospect a chance to talk.

Where the 'rinky-dinks' fall down
Rinky-dinks are the 'no problem' merchants who agree to anything to clinch a deal. Don't join their ranks. Whatever you promise in your presentation, you must always deliver, even if it costs you.

Asking for decisions in the public sector
This is a tricky one. A positive reaction or a verbal 'yes' in the public sector does not necessarily signify that written confirmation to proceed with be automatically forthcoming. The due process takes time (sometimes interminable) and priorities can change. It's often easier to negotiate and obtain 'notional' approval on your tender invitation or contract sanction, and then to exercise patience in the extreme while awaiting receipt of that vital piece of paper to solidify the deal.

TEN GOLDEN RULES TO OBSERVE

1. Master public sector selling procedures.

2. Always make preparation in advance of sales pitches.

3. Listen and take note.

4. Never deviate from the purpose of the meeting.

5. Never promise what you can't deliver.

6. Handle dissension with calm professionalism.

7. Stay cool when it all goes wrong.

8. Prepare well for pressurised selling negotiations.

9. Always project the essential you.

10. Do the deal, walk away and then get on with it.

CASE STUDY

'How many people do you employ?' asked the procurement officer.

'None, apart from the wife who looks after my admin on a part-time basis,' answered Jack.

'I see . . .' commented the official doubtfully. 'So in effect, you really *are* a sole trader?'

'That's right. I don't have tradesmen on the payroll, but I call upon a pool of experienced painters, plumbers, sparks and the like when-ever I need them. They're all time served, good workers, and unem-ployed like I was until I set up Jack of All Trades a year ago.'

'You'll appreciate, I'm sure,' said the procurement officer, 'that although this is a minor works project, reliability of labour and strict adherence to timescales is vital to us at the Ministry of Defence. Can you rely on your casual labour force?'

'I've been using these guys on a regular basis since I started and I've never once been let down by any of them.'

Jack's honesty and his preparation in advance for the sales pitch paid off. His wife informed him on his return to the yard that she'd had a telephone call informing her that a local purchase order for the project was going off in the post that very night.

EXERCISE

You've never done any public sector business before, you haven't even been invited to tender. Now you're going after some and you've made a start by fixing up an appointment with a council buyer to have a preliminary chat and establish whether there might be any openings for you either now or in the future.

Do your homework by drawing up a strategy for the pitch. Find out who they currently use and what they buy in your field, determine what you have to offer, and prepare a mini mission statement on why they should consider your services.

10

Adapting to New Ways

Selling to the public sector is a whole new experience and while at first you may find it strange, stick with it, adapt to the new ways, and soon you will feel you've been doing it all your working life. Many entrepreneurs discover that it gives them an added edge in their private sector dealings because of the extra dimension created by new knowledge, new perspectives and new insights into the global marketplace encompassing both cultures.

KEEPING ABREAST OF DEVELOPMENTS

Changes and developments occur rapidly in the public sector as a result of swings in public tastes, preferences and attitudes, and developments such as new laws. Keep abreast of these changes and developments by strict adherence to your daily information gathering: newspapers, television, business magazines, government and local authority journals . . . and the Internet.

You have many acts to perform in your working day but find a little time, no matter how busy you are, to maintain your information gathering. A good practice is to keep a daily log of the little snippets that come your way: a notebook or, better still, a computer file.

- Keep up with the changes.
- Maintain your information gathering.
- Log new data in a notebook or computer file.

PLANNING AHEAD ON ALL YOUR PROJECTS

Planning makes perfect and when you plan ahead on all your projects, you become so familiar with the route that if diversions pull you off course temporarily you can always find your way back effortlessly.

Attention to planning and preparation places you in command when you're sourcing for opportunities, asking for an invitation to tender, negotiating a contract, or just stating your case to public sector officials with a view to inclusion on their list of potential tenderers.

Planning ahead need not and should not take up too much of your time because very soon you'll be doing it automatically in relation to all your endeavours.

- Preparation brings you back on course quickly.
- Plan ahead for every activity.
- Do it regularly and it becomes an automatic action.

MAKING PROSPECTING A DAILY ROUTINE

Daily prospecting for opportunity is what will do it for you in the long run. No matter how much you know about the public sector, the procedures for selling, tendering, and enacting contracts, you won't win many of the latter (and it might all turn out to be a waste of time) if you don't make it a daily routine to prospect.

As with planning ahead on projects, it will eat up very little of your time each day and after a while it will become second nature to you.

- Daily prospecting pays off in the long term.
- Failure to prospect wins no contracts.

WATCHING OUT FOR PROCEDURAL CHANGES

In keeping abreast with changes and developments in the public sector, watch out for any proposed modifications in selling procedures. These occur from time to time and may affect all government departments or just a few – but it might be the few with whom you are currently doing business. Keep an eye out too for any potential new access routes to doing business.

Government journals and their information services on the Internet are good for tracking such changes.

- Look out for proposed changes in selling procedures – they might affect you.
- Track such modifications in government journals and the Internet.
- Look out for new access routes.

MAKING MARKETING A PRIME PRIORITY

Effective communication, good negotiation skills and the science of selling are all parts of the one essential whole: *marketing*. That's what the term 'marketing mix' *really* means.

Mixing advertising, promotions, public relations, etc on their own won't do it for you because they are only peripherals – but daily attention to the core aspects of the marketing mix will lead to success in your endeavours in the public sector.

We know what marketing is and what it is not, but always bear in mind that the first and most important piece of marketing you need to undertake is getting the best out of the essential you.

- Adopt the true marketing mix in your dealings.
- Attend to the first and most important piece of marketing activity.

DEVELOPING YOUR POWERS OF NEGOTIATION

Continue to develop your powers of negotiation so that when you are faced with difficult decisions and choices you will always be guided to walk in the right direction. Stay cool, calm, and collected in your negotiations and take note of the other party's points of view. This way you will be in command of the situation which is of course even more crucial in pressurised discussions.

- Face difficult decisions with confidence.
- Stay cool, calm and collected.
- Be in command in pressurised negotiations.

NEVER LOSE THE SELLING HABIT

Make selling your goods or services a personal remit and don't be tempted to pass it on to anyone else. Employ assistance by all means, but stay at the helm yourself on leading edge negotiation and selling situations. There's no greater excitement in business than meeting people and selling professionally to them. Never lose the habit.

CONTINUING TO LEARN

Nothing stands still for long. Continue to learn and grow.

We've reached the end of *Selling to the Public Sector* but it's only the beginning for you. I have been there and done it all. So too can you. May the winds of good fortune be always at your back.

Glossary

Access routes. The way in to doing business in the public sector (see Chapter 6).

Alert Service. A valuable service provided by EuroInfoCentres which offers updates on new and amended guidelines, regulations and legislation, as they affect the private sector.

Best-to-worst scenarios. The core element of a SWOT analysis: devising hypothetical scenarios as they might relate to the eventual outcome of a real situation.

Better Government. The initiative that looks at government from the point of view of the citizen and the business community; making it more effective, swifter, more accessible and easier to approach.

Business Information Services (BIP). The electronic publishing organisation which provides information on new public sector contract opportunities and which produces publications such as *Government Opportunities*, *Contrax Weekly*, *Defence Contracts*, etc.

Business Co-operation Service. The facility available free of charge at EuroInfoCentres for sourcing business partners on their electronic network of over 400 correspondents in Europe and beyond.

'Buying' assignments. The dangerous practice of cutting prices to an unacceptable level in order to obtain public sector business. When employed indiscriminately, this can result in downsizing overall profitability.

Call-off contracts. Contracts so constructed that the buyer, although committed to the eventual purchase of an agreed amount of stock, draws only from stockholding (and pays for) as and when required during the period of the contract.

Central government. Comprises the 48 ministries and departments responsible for serving the needs of the nation.

Central Office of Information (COI). The government executive agency that provides publicity and media relations services to government departments and publicly funded organisations.

Central Unit on Procurement (CUP). The division of HM Treasury which provides government departments with guidelines on purchasing and supply procedures and practices.

Citizen's Charter. Government initiative which was launched to raise the standard of public services and make them more accessible to end users, ie citizens of the United Kingdom.

Collections. The 14 regional offices of HM Customs and Excise.

Compulsory Competitive Tendering (CCT). The requirement on all government departments to test the quality of in-house enabling facilities through invitations to tender (ITTs) issued to private sector sources.

Contrax Weekly. The electronic publication which announces contract opportunities for the supply of goods and services to central and local government departments.

Contract management. The process which sets out to ensure that all parties to a public sector contract understand their respective obligations, enabling these to be carried out effectively and efficiently.

Considered purchases. The Central Unit of Procurement edict that requires government buyers and suppliers alike to recognise that all purchases are **considered purchases** in the quest for value-for-money transactions.

Creative negotiation. Employing all the practical elements of strategic negotiation to effect an acceptable outcome.

Cue sheet. Used as an aide-memoire in telephone negotiations.

Defence Export Services Organisation (DESO). This division of the Ministry of Defence complements the wider export services offered by the DTI.

Devolved budgeting system. The system that delegates authority to public sector procurement officers so that they can buy direct from suppliers without going through headquarters.

District councils. Local authorities with limited powers of responsibility in the provision of public services.

Defence Suppliers Service (DSS). The organisation which provides information and assistance to the private sector on all matters relating to Ministry of Defence contracts.

Enabling facilities. In the context of the public sector, this refers to those authorities that have the means to carry out certain service functions in-house.

EuroInfoCentres. The European Commission initiative which provides a network of over 230 centres giving access to all aspects of information of relevance to the business community.

Executive Agencies. The new service agencies designed to assist government in the fulfilment of its responsibilities.

Eyes on – hands off. The policy adopted by the Ministry of Defence with regard to the contractual activities of their prime suppliers, ie leaving with them the responsibility of appointing sub-contractors.

Financially free standing projects. Where the private sector undertakes DBFO, recovering costs from the end users ie tolling.

Government Information Service (GIS).The UK government web site which (in compliance with the Citizens Charter) openly relays on the Internet information relating to its policies and activities.

Government Purchasing Agency (GPA). The specialist unit with responsibility for purchasing activities across designated Ministries, Departments, Northern Ireland Civil Service Departments and the Northern Ireland Office.

Government auctions. Auction sales of government surplus, confiscated goods etc; held at various venues and at regular intervals throughout the United

Kingdom.

Grantfinder. The EuroInfoCentres electronic system designed to provide information on European and UK grant schemes.

Hidden agenda. Undisclosed motive for calling a meeting; motive that does not appear on the official agenda.

Intervention Board. The Next Steps Agency, which implements EC legislation regulating the market for many agricultural products and foodstuffs.

Intuitive techniques. Using native intuition as a means of determining problematic situations.

Invitations to tender (ITTs). The issuing of invitations to tender for public sector contracts; issued by procurement officers to suitable private sector concerns.

Joint ventures. Where two or more parties join forces to effect synergies across the spectrum of activities involved in a given project.

Local authorities. District, unitary, borough, county, city councils.

Local Enterprise Companies (LECs). Government sponsored quangos charged with the responsibility of regenerating the Scottish economy and fostering employment skills training.

Local purchases. Purchases sanctioned by managers of local governmental units where there is no requirement to process these through headquarters.

Local Government Association (LGA). The national voice for local communities which represents 500 authorities with a total population of 50 million people throughout England and Wales, spending £65 billion a year.

Lower value orders. Public sector purchasing orders valued at less than the prescribed threshold requiring participation in the tendering process.

Market testing. The element of Compulsory Competitive Tendering (CCT) that requires the public sector to market test value for money from in-house enabling facilities against what the private sector has to offer, issuing invitations to tender.

Marketing mix. The core aspects of marketing as opposed to peripherals such as advertising and promotion.

Match-and-match. The procedure adopted by procurement officers in matching the critical requirements of a consultancy project to the expertise of a specialist.

Matching requirements. Ensuring that no assignment is undertaken unless (a) it is within the capabilities of the contractor, and (b) it will produce an acceptable level of profit.

Meet-the-buyer events. Exhibitions and seminars where public sector buying organisations are in evidence as exhibitors or delegates.

Mission statement. A succinct written statement which highlights the key objectives of a given undertaking.

Ministry of Defence (MoD). The single biggest purchaser of goods and services in the public sector.

Model forms of contract. The three types of contract used by public sector buyers for purchasing goods, general services and consultancy expertise.

Negotiation strategies. The preparation (in advance of meetings) of relevant, effective strategies in order to ensure acceptable outcomes in face-to-face negotiation.

Next Steps Programme. The programme which launched the executive agencies to improve government and deliver better services within available resources.

Notional approval. Obtaining commitment in principle prior to the issue of a contract for providing the public sector with goods or services.

Personal presentation. The art of presenting in negotiation or face-to-face selling situations.

Private Finance Initiative (PFI). Where the private sector trades a wide range of commercial skills to the improved delivery of public services.

Precautionary policies. Procedures adopted by public sector buyers to ensure value for money in their transactional interfaces.

Pressurised negotiations. Where discussions reach a delicate stage, eg project running behind schedule; late delivery of merchandise; sub-contractors work below standard, etc.

Prime contractor. The term applied to major or 'favoured' contractors to the public sector.

Procurement directives. Directives on purchasing emanating from the EC and implemented into UK law.

Prompt Payers Code. The regulation which requires approved invoices to be cleared by the public sector within 30 days of receipt.

Protecting margins. Doing everything possible to maintain an acceptable level of profitability in public sector transactions; avoiding the downsizing of overall net margins.

Proven strategies. The strategies discussed in this book; strategies to ensure successful dealings with the public sector.

Projects. The term used by the Defence Estates Organisation (DEO) to define construction contracts with a value in excess of £240,000.

Project management. Where the DOE appoints a private concern to act as project manager with responsibility for the entire construction process from procurement through design to site supervision and handover.

Prospecting. The practice of ongoing sourcing for invitations to tender for public sector contracts.

Public sector. The overall structure of central and local government, responsible for serving the needs of the community.

Public sector marketplace. The government departments which purchase goods and services from the private sector.

Public/private partnerships. This concept is a government initiative to foster more flexible contractual relationships in achieving best value.

Publications orderline. The DTI contact point for requisitioning literature relating to matters of trade and commerce.

Quality assurance. The responsibility imposed by the public sector on prime contractors to maintain quality assurance by complying with the requirements of BS EN ISO 9001.

Regional government. The governing activities of local authorities.

Remit. An area of authority or competence in the public sector.

Resource accounting. An initiative to create an area of accounting and budgeting in the public sector similar to that which pertains in the private sector.

Scanfax. One of the scanning services operated by the Stationery Office; a service that will fax extracts from the *Official Journal of the European Communities* to subscribing customers.

Scattergun. The act of spreading information far and wide, eg a marketing campaign which uses disparate media to reach various socio-economic groups.

Selling-to guides. The range of booklets emanating from various government departments offering advice on how to sell to the public sector.

Selective press relations. Using government sponsored media selectively to obtain useful PR coverage.

Selling procedures. The range of procedures detailed in this book; procedures which must be mastered to trade effectively in the public sector.

Setting up your stall. Exhaustive preparation before embarking on public sector selling.

Single source contracts. Where one concern undertakes to perform all the tasks involved in a contractual obligation.

Sponsored publishing. An aspect of publishing where local authorities receive an agreed number of copies of a publication free of charge in return for exclusive advertising rights bestowed upon the publisher.

Structure of government. The various tiers of central and local government.

Suppliers Charter. The charter administered by the Government Purchasing Agency which provides for suppliers to compete in fair and open competition for the provision of goods and services to the public sector.

Tenders Electronic Daily (TED). The electronic version of the *Official Journal of the European Communities (OJ)* which provides daily updates on public sector contract opportunities throughout Europe.

Tender. An offer to provide goods or services.

Tendering criteria. The basic conditions set out to satisfy the requirements of an invitation to tender.

Term commission. The provision of advisory services to the Defence Works Advisor; services which involve initial assessment, order of cost estimates, option studies, condition surveys and preparation of brief.

Training and Enterprise Councils (TECs). Government sponsored quangos charged to regenerate the economies of England and Wales and to foster employment skills training.

Unitary Councils. Those local authorities with comprehensive powers of responsibility in the provision of public services.

Win-win. The core element of negotiation strategy; something for all parties concerned in a discussion.

Appendix

CENTRAL GOVERNMENT DEPARTMENTS

Advisory, Conciliation and Arbitration Service (ACAS)
Ministry of Agriculture, Fisheries and Food (MAFF)
Biotechnology and Biological Sciences Research Council (BBSRC)
British Library
Buying Agency
Cabinet Office
Central Computer and Telecommunications Agency (CCTA)
Central Office of Information (COI)
Council for the Central Laboratory of the Research Council (CCLRC)
The Court Service
Crown Prosecution Service (CPS)
Welsh Historic Monuments (CADW)
HM Customs and Excise
Ministry of Defence (MoD)
Department for Education and Employment (DfEE)
Employment Service (ES)
Department of the Environment
Export Credits Guarantee Department (ECGD)
Foreign and Commonwealth Office (FCO)
Department of Health
Health and Safety Executive (HSE)
Home Office
Inland Revenue
Intervention Board
HM Land Registry
Metropolitan Police Force
Department of National Heritage
Department for National Savings
Natural Environment Research Council
Office for National Statistics
Office of Water Services (OFWAT)
Ordnance Survey
Overseas Development Administration (ODA)
UK Passport Agency
Public Records Office (PRO)
Royal Mint

Engineering and Physical Sciences Research Council (EPSRC)
Department of Social Security (DSS)
Department of Trade and Industry (DTI)
Department of Transport
HM Treasury
The Treasury Solicitor
Northern Ireland
The Scottish Office
Welsh Office
National Health Service (NHS)
Higher Education Institutions
Local Authorities

Chapter 6 contains a complete list of addresses for all central government departments.

EXECUTIVE AGENCIES

Agencies of the Ministry of Agriculture, Fisheries and Food
Agriculture Development and Advisory Service (ADAS)
Central Science Laboratory
Intervention Board
Meat Hygiene Service
Pesticides Safety Directorate
Veterinary Laboratories Agency
Veterinary Medicines Directorate

Agency of the Attorney General
Government Property Lawyers

Agencies of the Chancellor of the Exchequer
Central Statistical Office
Paymaster
Royal Mint
Valuation Office

Agencies of the Secretary of State for Defence
Army Base Repair Organisation
Army Base Storage and Distribution Agency
Army Technical Support Agency
Defence Analytical Services Agency
Defence Animal Centre
Defence Bills Agency
Defence Clothing and Textiles Agency
Defence Evaluation and Research Agency

Defence Postal and Courier Services
Defence Transport and Movements Executive
Disposal Sales Agency
Duke of York's Royal Military School
Hydrographic Office
Logistic Information Systems Agency
Meteorological Office
Military Survey
Naval Aircraft Repair Organisation
Naval Recruiting and Training Agency
Pay and Personnel Agency
Queen Victoria School
RAF Maintenance Group Defence Agency
RAF Signals Engineering Establishment
RAF Training Group Defence Agency
Service Children's Schools (North West Europe)

Agencies of the Secretary of State for Education and Employment
Employment Service
Teachers' Pension Agency

Agencies of the Secretary of State for the Environment
Building Research Establishment
The Buying Agency
Ordnance Survey
Planning Inspectorate
Queen Elizabeth II Conference Centre
Security Facilities Executive

Agency of the Secretary of State for Foreign and Commonwealth Affairs
Wilton Park

Agencies for the Secretary of State for Health
Medical Devices Agency
Medicines Control Agency
NHS Estates
NHS Pensions Agency

Agencies of the Home Secretary
Fire Service College
Forensic Science Service

HM Prison Service
UK Passport Agency

Agencies of the Lord Chancellor
Court Service
HM Land Registry
Public Record Office
Public Trust Office

Agencies of the Secretary of State for National Heritage
Historic Royal Palaces Agency
Royal Parks Agency

Agencies of the Secretary of State for Northern Ireland
Compensation Agency
Driver and Vehicle Licensing (Northern Ireland)
Driver and Vehicle Testing Agency
Forensic Science Agency of Northern Ireland
Industrial Research and Technology Unit
Northern Ireland Child Support Agency
Northern Ireland Health and Social Services Estates Agency
Northern Ireland Prison Service
Ordnance Survey of Northern Ireland
Public Record Office of Northern Ireland
Rate Collection Agency
Social Security Agency (Northern Ireland)
Training and Employment Agency (Northern Ireland)
Valuation and Lands Agency

Agency for the Minister of Overseas Development
Natural Resources Institute

Agencies of the Chancellor of the Duchy of Lancaster and Minister for Public Service
Central Office of Information
Chessington Computer Centre
Civil Service College
HMSO
Occupational Health and Safety Agency
Recruitment and Assessment Services Agency

Agencies of the Secretary of State for Scotland
Historic Scotland
Registers of Scotland

Scottish Agricultural Science Agency
Scottish Court Service
Scottish Fisheries Protection Agency
Scottish Office Pensions Agency
Scottish Prison Service
Scottish Record Office
Student Awards Agency for Scotland

Agencies for the Secretary of State for Social Security
Social Security Benefits Agency
Social Security Child Support Agency
Social Security Contributions Agency
Social Security Information Technology Services Agency
Social Security Resettlement Agency
Social Security War Pensions Agency

Agencies of the Secretary of State for Trade and Industry
Companies House
Insolvency Service
Laboratory of the Government Chemist
National Weights and Measures Laboratory
Patent Office
Radiocommunications Agency

Agencies of the Secretary of State for Transport
Coastguard
Driver and Vehicle Licensing Agency
Driving Standards Agency
Highways Agency
Marine Safety Agency
Transport Research Laboratory
Vehicle Certification Agency
Vehicle Inspectorate

Agency of the Secretary of State for Wales
CADW: Welsh Historic Monuments

Refer to the publication *A Guide to the Executive Agencies* for location details.

UK LOCAL AUTHORITIES

Key
C – county councils (England)
CI – Channels Islands
D – district council (England)
EU – unitary council (England)
IoMB – Isle of Man borough
IoM – Isle of Man
LB – London borough
MB – Metropolitan borough
NID – Northern Ireland district
SU – unitary council (Scotland)
WU – unitary council (Wales)

A
Aberdeen City SU
Aberdeenshire SU
Adur D
Alderney CI
Allerdale D
Alnwick D
Amber Valley D
Angus SU
Antrim NID
Ards NID
Argyll and Bute SU
Armagh NID
Ashfield D
Aylesbury Vale D

B
Babergh D
Ballymena NID
Ballymoney NID
Banbridge NID
Barking and
   Dagenham LB
Barnet LB
Barnsley MB
Barrow-in-Furness D
Basildon D
Basingstoke and Deane
   D
Bassetlaw D
Bath and North East

Somerset EU
Bedford D
Bedfordshire C
Belfast NID
Berkshire C
Berwick-upon-Tweed D
Bexley LB
Birmingham MB
Blaby D
Blackburn with
   Darwen EU
Blackpool EU
Blaenau Gwent WU
Blyth Valley D
Bolsover D
Bolton MB
Boston D
Bournemouth EU
Bracknell Forest EU
Bradford MB
Braintree D
Breckland D
Brent LB
Brentwood D
Bridgend WU
Bridgnorth D
Brighton and Hove EU
Bristol EU
Broadland D
Bromley LB
Bromsgrove D
Broxbourne D

Broxtowe D
Buckinghamshire C
Burnley D
Bury MB

C
Caerphilly WU
Calderdale MB
Cambridge D
Cambridgeshire C
Camden LB
Cannock Chase D
Canterbury D
Caradon D
Cardiff WU
Carlisle D
Camarthenshire WU
Carrick D
Carrickfergus NID
Castle Morpeth D
Castle Point D
Castlereagh NID
Castletown
   Commissioners IoM
Ceredigion WU
Channel Islands
Charnwood D
Chelmsford D
Cheltenham D
Cherwell D
Cheshire C

Chester D
Chester-le-Street D
Chesterfield D
Chichester D
Chiltern D
Chorley D
Christchurch D
City and County of
    Swansea WU
City of Edinburgh SU
City of Glasgow SU
City of York EU
Clackmannanshire SU
Colchester D
Coleraine NID
Congleton D
Conwy WU
Cookstown NID
Copeland D
Corby D
Corporation of London
Cornwall C
Cotswold D
Coventry MB
Craigavon NID
Craven D
Crawley D
Crewe and Nantwich D
Croydon LB
Cumbria C

D

Dacorum D
Darlington EU
Dartford D
Daventry D
Denbighshire WU
Derby EU
Derbyshire Dales D
Derry NID
Derwentside D
Devon C
Doncaster MB
Dorset C
Douglas IoMB
Dover D

Down NID
Dudley MB
Dumfries & Galloway
    SU
Dundee City SU
Dungannon NID
Durham C
Durham D

E

Ealing LB
Easington D
East Ayrshire SU
Eastbourne D
East Cambridge D
East Devon D
East Dorset D
East Dunbartonshire
    SU
East Hampshire D
East Hertfordshire D
Eastleigh D
East Lindsay D
East Lothian SU
East Northamptonshire
    D
East Renfrewshire SU
East Riding of
    Yorkshire EU
East Staffordshire D
East Sussex C
Eden D
Ellesmere Port and
    Neston D
Elmbridge D
Enfield LB
Epping Forest D
Epsom and Ewell D
Erewash D
Essex C
Exeter D

F

Falkirk SU
Fareham D
Fenland D

Fermanagh NID
Fife SU
Flintshire WU
Forest Heath D
Forest of Dean D
Fylde D

G

Gateshead MB
Gedling D
Gillingham D
Gloucester D
Gloucestershire C
Gosport D
Gravesham D
Great Yarmouth D
Greenwich LB
Guernsey CI
Guildford D
Gwynedd WU

H

Hackney LB
Halton EU
Hambleton D
Hammersmith and
    Fulham LB
Hampshire C
Harborough D
Haringey LB
Harlow D
Harrogate D
Harrow LB
Hart D
Hartlepool EU
Hastings D
Havant D
Havering LB
Herefordshire EU
Hereford and
    Worcester C
Herm C
Hertfordshire EU
Hertsmere D
Highland SU
High Peak D

Hillingdon LB
Hinckley and Bosworth D
Horsham D
Hounslow LB
Huntingdonshire D
Hyndburn D

I

Inverclyde SU
Ipswich D
Isle of Anglesey WU
Isle of Man IoM
Isle of Wight EU
Isles of Scilly
Islington LB

J

Jersey CI
Jethou CI

K

Kennet D
Kensington and Chelsea LB
Kent C
Kerrier D
Kettering D
Kings Lynn and West Norfolk D
Kingston upon Hull EU
Kingston upon Thames LB
Kirklees MB
Knowsley MB

L

Lambeth LB
Lancashire C
Lancaster D
Larne NID
Laxey Village Commissioners IoM
Leeds MB
Leicester EU

Leicestershire C
Lewes D
Lewisham LB
Lichfield D
Limavady NID
Lincoln D
Lincolnshire C
Lisburn NID
Liverpool MB
Londonderry NID
Luton EU

M

Macclesfield D
Magherfelt NID
Maidstone D
Maldon D
Malvern Hills D
Manchester MB
Mansfield D
Medway Towns EU
Melton D
Mendip D
Merthyr Tydfil WU
Merton LB
Michael Village Commissioners IoM
Mid Bedfordshire D
Mid Devon D
Middlesborough EU
Midlothian SU
Mid Suffolk D
Mid Sussex D
Milton Keynes EU
Mole Valley D
Monmouthshire WU
Moray SU
Moyle NID

N

Neath Port Talbot WU
Newark and Sherwood D
Newbury EU
Newcastle under Lyme D

Newcastle upon Tyne MB
New Forest D
Newham LB
Newport WU
Newry and Mourne NID
Newtonabbey NID
Norfolk C
Northampton D
Northamptonshire C
North Ayrshire SU
North Cornwall D
North Devon D
North Dorset D
North Down NID
North East Derbyshire D
North East Lincolnshire EU
North Hertfordshire D
North Kesteven D
North Lanarkshire SU
North Lincolnshire EU
North Norfolk D
North Shropshire D
North Somerset EU
North Tyneside MB
Northumberland C
North Warwickshire D
North West Leicestershire D
North Wiltshire D
North Yorkshire C
Norwich D
Nottingham EU
Nottinghamshire C
Nuneaton and Bedworth D

O

Oadby and Wigston D
Oldham MB
Omagh NID
Onchan Commissioners IoM

Orkney SU
Oswestery D
Oxford D
Oxfordshire C

P
Peel Town
   Commissioners IoM
Pembrokeshire WU
Pendle D
Penwith D
Perth and Kinross SU
Peterborough EU
Plymouth EU
Poole EU
Port Erin
   Commissioners IoM
Portsmouth EU
Port St Mary
   Commissioners IoM
Powys WU
Preston D
Purbeck D

R
Ramsey Town
   Commissioners IoM
Reading EU
Redbridge LB
Redcar and Cleveland
   EU
Redditch D
Reigate and Barnstead
   D
Renfrewshire SU
Restormel D
Rhondda Cynon Taff
   WU
Ribble Valley D
Richmondshire D
Richmond upon
   Thames LB
Rochdale MB
Rochester upon
   Medway D

Rochford D
Rossendale D
Rother D
Rotherham MB
Rugby D
Runnymede D
Rushcliffe D
Rushmoor D
Rutland EU
Ryedale D

S
St Albans D
St Edmundbury D
St Helens MB
Salford MB
Salisbury D
Sandwell MB
Sark CI
Scarborough D
Scottish Borders SU
Sedgefield D
Sedgemoor D
Sefton MB
Selby D
Sevenoaks D
Sheffield MB
Shepway D
Shetland SU
Shrewsbury and
   Atchan D
Shropshire C
Slough EU
Solihull EU
Somerset C
Southampton EU
South Ayrshire SU
South Bedfordshire D
South Bucks D
South Cambridgeshire
   D
South Derbyshire D
Southend-on-Sea EU
South Gloucestershire
   EU
South Hams D

South Holland D
South Kesteven D
South Lakeland D
South Lanarkshire SU
South Norfolk D
South
   Northamptonshire D
South Oxfordshire D
South Ribble D
South Shropshire D
South Somerset D
South Staffordshire D
South Tyneside MB
Southwark LB
Spelthorne D
Stafford D
Staffordshire C
Staffordshire
   Moorlands D
Stevenage D
Stirling SU
Stockport MB
Stockton-on-Tees EU
Stoke-on-Trent EU
Strabane NID
Stratford-on-Avon D
Stroud D
Suffolk C
Suffolk Coastal D
Sunderland MB
Surrey C
Surrey Heath D
Sutton LB
Swale D
Swindon EU

T
Tameside MB
Tamworth D
Tunbridge D
Taunton Deane D
Teesdale D
Teignbridge D
Tendring D
Test Valley D
Tewkesbury D

Thanet D
Three Rivers D
Thurrock EU
Tonbridge and Malling D
Torbay EU
Torfaen WU
Torridge D
Tower Hamlets LB
Trafford MB
Tunbridge Wells D
Tynedale D

U
Uttlesford D

V
Vale of Glamorgan WU
Vale of White Horse D
Vale Royal D

W
Wakefield MB
Walsall MB

Waltham Forest LB
Wandsworth LB
Wansbeck D
Warrington EU
Warwick D
Warwickshire C
Watford D
Waveney D
Waverley D
Wealdon D
Wear Valley D
Wellingborough D
Welwyn Hatfield D
West Devon D
West Dorset D
West Dunbartonshire SU
West Lancashire D
West Lindsay D
West Lothian SU
Westminster LB
West Oxfordshire D
West Somerset D
West Sussex C
West Wiltshire D

Western Isles SU
Weymouth and Portland D
Wigan MB
Wiltshire C
Winchester D
Windsor and Maidenhead D
Wirral MB
Woking D
Wokingham EU
Wolverhampton MB
Worcester D
Worcestershire C
Worthing D
Wrekin (The) EU
Wrexham WU
Wychavon D
Wycombe D
Wrye D
Wrye Forest D

Refer to the publication *Municipal Yearbook and Public Services Directory* for location details.

Useful Addresses

TRAINING AND ENTERPRISE COUNCILS

England and Wales

Avon TEC, St Lawrence House, Broad Street, Bristol BS99.

AZTEC, 2 Manorgate Road, Kingston-upon-Thames, KT2 7AL.

Barnsley/Doncaster TEC, Conference Centre, Eldon Street, Barnsley S70 2JL.

Bedfordshire TEC, Woburn Court, 2 Railton Road, Woburn Industrial Estate, Kempston MK42 7PN.

Birmingham TEC, Chaplin Court, 80 Hurst Street, Birmingham B5 4TG.

Bolton Bury TEC, Clive House, Clive Street, Bolton BL1 1ET.

Bradford and District TEC, Fountain Hall, Fountain Street, Bradford BD1 3RA.

Calderdale/Kirklees TEC, Park View House, Woodvale Office Park, Brighouse HD6 4AB.

CAMBSTEC (Central and South Cambridgeshire), Trust Court, Chivers Way, The Vision Park, Histon CB4 4PW.

Central England TEC, The Oaks, Clewes Road, Redditch B98 7ST.

CENTEC (Central London), 12 Grosvenor Crescent, London SW1X 7EE.

CEWTEC (Chester, Ellesmere Port, Wigan), Woodside Business Park, Birkenhead, Wirral L41 1EH.

CILNTEC (City and Inner London North), 89 Great Eastern Road, London EC2A 3DP.

County Durham TEC, Valley Street North, Darlington DL1 1TJ.

Coventry and Warwickshire TEC, Brandon Court, Progress Way, Coventry CV3 2TE.

Cumbria TEC, Venture House, Regents Court, Guard Street, Workington CA14 4EW.

Devon and Cornwall TEC, Foliot House, Budshead Road, Crownhill, Plymouth PL6 5XR.

Dorset TEC, 25 Oxford Road, Bournemouth BH8 8EY.

Dudley TEC, Dudley Court South, Waterfront East, Level Street, Brierley Hill DY5 1XN.

ELTEC (East Lancashire), Red Rose Court, Clayton Business Park, Clayton-le-Moor BB5 5JR.

Essex TEC, Redwing House, Hedgerows Business Park, Colchester Road, Chelmsford CM2 5PB.

Gloucestershire TEC, Conway House, Worcester Road, Gloucester GL1 3AJ.

Greater Nottingham TEC, Castle Marina Park, Nottingham NG7 1TN.

Greater Peterborough TEC, Blenheim Court, Peppercorn Close, Peterborough PE1 2DU.

Gwent TEC, Glyndwr Road, Cleppa Park, Newport NP9 1YE.

Hampshire TEC, 25 Thackeray Mall, Fareham PO16 0PQ.

HAWTEC (Hereford and Worcester), Haswell House, St Nicholas Street, Worcester WR1 1UW.

Heart of England TEC, The Quadrant, Abingdon Science Park, Abingdon OX14 3YS.

Hertfordshire TEC, 45 Grosvenor Road, ST Albans AL1 3AW.

Humberside TEC, The Maltings, Silvester Square, Hull HU1 3HL.

Kent TEC, Mountbatten House, 28 Military Road, Chatham ME4 4JE.

LAWTEC (Lancashire Area West), Duchy House, 96 Lancaster Road, Preston PR1 1HE.

Leeds TEC, Belgrave Hall, Belgrave Street, Leeds LS2 8DD.

Leicestershire TEC, Meridian Business Park, Leicester LE3 2WZ.

Lincolnshire TEC, Beech House, Witham Park, Waterside South, Lincoln LN5 7JH.

London East TEC, Cityside House, 40 Alder Street, London E1 1EE.

Manchester TEC, Boulton House, Chorlton Street, Manchester M1 3HY.

Merseyside TEC, Tithebarn House, Tithebarn Street, Liverpool L2 2NZ.

METROTEC (Wigan), Buckingham Row, Northway, Wigan WN1 1XX.

Mid Glamorgan TEC, Mains Avenue, Treforest Industrial Estate, Pontypridd CF37 5YL.

Milton Keynes and North Buckinghamshire TEC, Old Market Halls, Creed Street, Wolverton MK12 5LY.

Norfolk and Waveney TEDC, Norwich Business Park, Whiting Road, Norwich NR4 6DJ.

NORMIDTEC (North and Mid Cheshire), Spencer House, Dewhurst Road, Birchwood, Warrington WA3 7PP.

North Derbyshire TEC, St Mary's Court, St Mary's Gate, Chesterfield S41 7TD.

North East Wales TEC, Hightown Barracks, Kingsmill Road, Wrexham LL13 8BH.

North London TEC, Dumayne House, Fox Lane, Palmers Green, London N13 4AB.

North Nottinghamshire TEC, Edwinstowe House, High Street Edwinstowe, Mansfield NG21 9PR.

North West London TEC, Kirkfield House, Station Road, Harrow HA1 2RL.

North Yorkshire TEC, TEC House, Pioneer Business Park, Amy Johnson Way, Clifton Moorgate, York YO3 8TN.

Northamptonshire TEC, Royal Pavilion, Moulton Park Industrial Estate, Northampton NN3 1WD.

Northumberland TEC, Craster Court, Cramlington NE23 6XX.

Oldham TEC, Meridian Centre, King Street, Oldham OL8 1EZ.

Powys TEC, St David's House, Newtown, Powys SY16 1RB.

QUALITEC (St Helens), Waterside Court, Technology Campus, St Helens WA9 1UE.

Rochdale TEC, St James Place, Yorkshire Street, Rochdale OL16 2DL.

Rotherham TEC, Moorgate House, Moorgate Road, Rotherham S60 2EN.

Sandwell TEC, Kingston House, High Street, West Bromwich B70 9LD.

Sheffield TEC, St Mary's Court, St Mary's Road, Sheffield S2 4AQ.

Shropshire TEC, Hazledine House, Central Square, Telford TF3 4JJ

SOLOTEC, Lancaster House, 7 Elmfield Road, Bromley BR1 1LT.

Somerset TEC, Crescent House, The Mount, Taunton TA1 3TT.

South and East Cheshire TEC, Middlewich Industrial and Business Park, Dalton Way, Middlewich CW10 0HU.

South Glamorgan TEC, Drakes Walk, Waterfront 2000, Atlantic Wharf, Cardiff CF1 5AN.

South Thames TEC, 200 Great Dover Street, London SE1 4YB.

Southern Derbyshire TEC, St Helens Court, St Helens Street, Derby DE1 3GY.

Staffordshire TEC, Festival Park, Stoke on Trent ST1 5TQ.

Stockport/High Peak TEC, St Peters Square, Stockport SK1 1NN.

Suffolk TEC, Crown House, Crown Street, Ipswich IP1 3HS.

Surrey TEC, Technology House, Goldsworth Road, Woking GU12 1LE.

Sussex House TEC, Electrowatt House, North Street, Horsham RH12 1RS.

TARGED (North West Wales), Llys Britannia, Parc Menai, Bangor LL57 4BN.

Teeside TEC, Training and Enterprise House, Queens Square, Middlesborough TS2 1AA.

Thames Valley Enterprise, Kings Point, 120 Kings Road, Reading RG1 3BZ.

Tyneside TEC, Moongate House, 5th Avenue Business Park, Team Valley Trading Estate, Gateshead NE11 0HF.

Wakefield TEC, Grove Hall, College Grove Road, Wakefield WF1 3RN.

Walsall TEC, Townend House, Townend Square, Walsall WS1 1NS.

Wearside TEC, Derwent House, New Town Centre, Washington NE38 7ST.

West London TEC, Sovereign Court, Staines Road, Hounslow TW3 3HA.

West Wales TEC, Orchard House, Orchard Street, Swansea SA1 5DJ.

Wight Training and Enterprise, Mill Court, Furrlongs, Newport, Isle of Wight PO30 2AA.

Wiltshire TEC, The Bora Building, Westlea Campus, Westlea Down, Swindon SN5 7EZ.

Wolverhampton TEC, Pendeford Business Park, Wobaston Road, Wolverhampton WV9 5HA.

LOCAL ENTERPRISE COMPANIES

Scottish Enterprise Area

Forth Valley Enterprise, Laurel House, Laurelbank Business Park, Stirling FK7 9JQ.

Dunbartonshire Enterprise, Spectrum House, Clydebank Business Park,

Clydebank G81 2DR.

Renfrewshire Enterprise Company, Causeyside Street, Paisley PA1 1UL.

Glasgow Development Agency, Atrium Court, Waterloo Street, Glasgow G2 6HQ.

Enterprise Ayrshire, Hill Street, Kilmarnock KA3 1HA.

Dumfries and Galloway Enterprise, Cairnsmore House, Bank End Road, Dumfries DG1 4TA.

Grampian Enterprise, Albyn Place, Aberdeen AB1 1YI.

Scottish Enterprise Tayside, Enterprise House, North Lindsay Street, Dundee DD1 1HT.

Fife Enterprise, Huntsman's House, Cadham Centre, Glenrothes KY7 6RU.

Lothian and Edinburgh Enterprise Ltd, Apex House, Haymarket Terrace, Edinburgh EH12 5HD.

Scottish Borders Enterprise, Bridge Street, Galashiels TD1 1SW.

Lanarkshire Development Agency, New Lanarkshire House, Willow Drive, Strathclyde Business Park, Bellshill ML4 3GD.

Highlands and Islands Enterprise Areas

Moray, Badenoch and Strathspey Enterprise, Elgin Business Centre, Elgin IV30 1RH.

Inverness and Nairn Enterprise, Castle Wynd, Inverness IV2 3DW.

Shetland Enterprise, Toll Clock Shopping Centre, North Road, Lerwick ZE1 0PE.

Caithness and Sutherland Enterprise, Princess Street, Thurso KW14 7BQ.

Western Isles Enterprise, Harbour View, Cromwall Street Bay, Stornoway, Isle of Lewis PA88 5LA.

Skye and Lochalsh Enterprise, Bridge Road, Portree, Isle of Skye IV51 9ER.

Argyll and the Island Enterprise, Stag Chambers, Lorne Street, Lochgilphead PA31 8LU.

Orkney Enterprise, Queen Street, Kirkwall, Orkney KW15 1JW.

Ross and Cromarty Enterprise, High Street, Invergordon IV18 9DH.

UK NATIONAL PARKS

The Broads Authority, Thomas Harvey House, 18 Colegate, Norwich NR3 1BQ.

Brecon Beacons National Park Authority, 7 Glamorgan Street, Brecon, Powys LD3 7DP.

Darmoor National Park Authority, Parke, Haytor Road, Bovey Tracey, Newton Abbott, Devon TQ13 3JQ.

Exmoor National Park Authority, National Park Office, Exmoor House, Dulverton, Somerset TA22 9HL.

Lake District National Park Authority, Murley Moss, Oxenholme Road, Kendal, Cumbria LA9 7RL.

Northumberland National Park Authority, Eastburn, South Park, Hexham, Northumberland NE46 1BS.

North York Moors National Park Authority, The Old Vicarage, Bondgate, Helmsley, Yorkshire YO62 5BP.

Peak District National Park Authority, Aldern House, Baslow Road, Bakewell, Derbyshire DE45 1AE.

Pembrokeshire Coast National Park Authority, Winch Lane, Haverfordwest, Pembrokeshire SA61 1PY.

Snowdonia National Park Authority, Penrhyndeudraeth, Gwynedd LL48 6LF.

Yorkshire Dales National Park Authority, Yorebridge House, Bainbridge, Leyburn, North Yorkshire DL8 3BY.

TRADE ASSOCIATIONS

Confederation of British Industry, Centre Point, 103 Oxford Street, London WC1A 1DU. Tel: (020) 7379 7400.

Defence Manufacturers Association, Marlborough House, Headley Road, Grayshot, Hindhead GU26 6LG.

Defence Industries Council, 60 Petty France, Victoria, London SW1H 9EU. Tel: (020) 7227 1000.

Further Reading

PUBLIC SECTOR GUIDES

Municipal Yearbook and Public Services Directory. Lists the main contact points in councils throughout the United Kingdom. Available from Newman Books, 32 Vauxhall Bridge Road, London SW1V 2SS. Tel:(020) 7973 6400

Local Government Association Yearbook. Available from LGA, 26 Chapter Street, London SW1P 4ND. Tel: (020) 7664 3000.

A Guide to the Executive Agencies. Published by Carlton Publishing & Printing Ltd, Rayners Lane, Pinner, HA5 5DY. Tel: (020) 8429 0056.

PUBLIC SECTOR PUBLICATIONS

Government Opportunities. Available from Government Opportunities, BIP Freepost, Glasgow G3 6BR. Tel: (0141) 332 8247

Official Journal of the European Communities. Available from The Stationery Office Publications Centre, PO Box 276, London SW8 5DT. Tel: (020) 7873 9090 (individual copies). Tel: (020) 7873 8409 (subscriptions).

MoD Contracts Bulletin. Available from Business Information Publications Ltd, 15 Woodlands Terrace, Glasgow G3 6DF. Tel: (0141) 332 8247.

Defence Works Service Opportunities. Subscription details as for MoD Contracts Bulletin.

PUBLIC SECTOR 'SELLING TO' BOOKLETS

Selling to MAFF
Selling Through the Buying Agency
Selling to HM Customs and Excise
Selling to the Ministry of Defence
Selling to the DOE
A Suppliers' Guide (Home Office)

Suppliers' Guide for Selling to National Savings
Ordnance Survey – Suppliers' Guide
Selling to the Department of Transport
Selling to the Public Sector in Northern Ireland

See Chapter 6 for details on how to obtain these leaflets.

Index

access routes, 61
alert service, 30
appointments, making, 113
assessing goods and services, 24

best-to-worst scenarios, 109
Better Government, 17
Business Co-operation Service, 30
Business Information Publications (BiP), 44
'buying' assignments, 114

call-off contracts, 48
central government, 12
Central Computer and Telecommunications Agency (CCTA), 66
Central Office of Information (COI), 67
Central Unit on Procurement (CUP), 34
Citizens Charter, 96
collections, 69
commercial opportunities, 17
Compulsory Competitive Tendering (CCT), 17
considered purchases, 113
construction industry contracts, 57
consultancy services, 95
contract management, 48
Contrax Weekly, 44
creative negotiation, 102
cue sheet, 106

Defence Suppliers Service, 53
demands and constraints, 16
devolved budgeting system, 82
district council, 14

enabling facilities, 11
EuroInfoCentres, 29
executive agencies, 16
exhibitions, 67
exporting, 58
external marketing services, 18
eyes on – hands off policy, 56

face-to-face selling, 113

financially free standing projects, 42
fitness to purpose, 25

government auctions, 36
Government Information Service (GIS), 17
government publications, exploring, 29
Government Purchasing Agency (GPA), 46
Grantfinder, 30

hidden agenda, 102
hypermart of opportunity, 11

identifying appropriate markets, 21
information gathering, 23
Internet, 31
Intervention Board, 76
intuitive techniques, 115
invitations to tender (ITTs), 118

joint ventures, 42

lateral thinking, 26
local authorities, 14
local digest, 24
Local Enterprise Companies (LECs), 16
Local Government Association (LGA), 15
local purchases, 35
looking for opportunities, 28
lower value orders, 57

margins, protecting, 114
market intelligence, 30
market testing, 86
marketing a consultancy service, 95
marketing mix, 120
match-and-match, 95
matching requirements, 114
Meet-the-Buyer events, 47
meetings, handling, 101
Ministry of Defence (MoD), 52
mission statement, 18
model forms of contract, 34

national and local levels, 57
negotiating by telephone, 106
negotiating sub-contracts, 55
negotiation strategies, 99
new suppliers, 11
Next Steps Programme, 17
notional approval, 115

payment on time, 49
perceived value, 35
personal database, 32
personal presentation, 93
planning ahead, 21
precautionary policies, 96
preliminary planning strategy, 26
press relations, selective, 96
pressurised negotiations, 109
prime contractor, 54
Private Finance Initiative (PFI), 42
procurement directives, 41
project management, 57
projects, 57
promotion in the public sector, 93
prospecting, 113
public/private partnerships, 58
public sector administration, 12
public sector marketplace, 20
publications orderline, 42

quality assurance, 46

regional government, 16
remit, 56
resource accounting, 96

Scanfax, 44
scattergun, 18
selling to Europe, 50
selling-to guides, 29
selling procedures, 39
single source contracts, 29
sponsored publishing, 35, 94
strategies, proven, 61
streamlining, 16
structure of government, 11
Suppliers Charter, 47

ten golden rules, 116
tendering, 28, 34
    criteria, 34
    procedures, 15
Tenders Electronic Daily (TED), 30
term commission, 57
Training and Enterprise Councils
    (TECs), 16

Unitary Council, 15

win-win, 99